ROSES AND THORNS

RHYMES AND REFLECTIONS

In the warmth of a ray of sunlight
In the whisper of a breeze
Between the starlit heavens
And the deepest seas
There's a place that's called forever
Where each of us is born…
For there is no end to living
When into spirit we transform.

Unknown

This book is dedicated to:

My husband Tom, who has
Been standing by me for 45 years,
As I discovered who I was
And what I had to offer
The world.
That journey of discovery
Continues, because God
Isn't finished with me yet
And Tom is still enabling me
To become...

TABLE OF CONTENTS

Designates a poem *

TABLE OF ILLUSTRATIONS

PHOTOGRAPHS

WORDS

I hope these beautiful words that I write;
Might someday live in your heart in the night;
When fears and doubts fill you with dread;
I pray you'll recall these words I have said.

May the words of my heart and my thoughts, combined;
With the love of the Spirit come to your mind;
May they bring you wisdom and courage to live;
Everlasting peace and serenity give.

May they guide you and keep you until the last;
When you take a final look at the life that is past;
May you follow the footsteps others have trod;
Till you cross safely into the arms of your God.

Never alone in this world will you stand;
If in pain or in sorrow, you reach out your hand;
God's arms will enfold you at life's every turn;
His eyes of compassion upon you will burn.

God's endless love and forgiveness is all you will need;
When the storms of life cut you and leave you to bleed;
When darkness surrounds you, let love be your sight;
For darkness can't live in the Presence of Light.

Seek truth, love and beauty in all that you do;
And the blessings of heaven will rain down on you;
Be honest, be faithful, steadfast and strong;
From God you descended and to Him you belong.

J.S. Schmidt- May 12, 2019- Mother's Day

IN MY LIFE

As you open this book, you might be asking yourself; *"What value is there in reflection? Isn't it just rehashing the past and the past certainly can't be altered"* I would counter that argument by saying this: *It **is** possible to alter the past in this one respect; as time passes, perspective often changes and even the past, which seems set in stone, can sometimes be seen with new eyes.*

Often with the passage of time, details have emerged that alter what was once believed to be unalterable. When this occurs, new insights can appear that bring the past into much clearer focus. Many people and events from the past, upon reexamination, can be redeemed in the light of the present, as opposed to the way they appeared in a former time.

In my own life, I have made some fascinating discoveries, both positive and negative in nature, by taking time to reflect on the past. It is a way to come to know yourself as you've never experienced yourself before. Knowing yourself to a greater degree, helps you understand others in a much deeper context. You begin to see the ways in which we are all the same and to have a greater appreciation for our differences. It allows you to see the actions of others toward yourself with a greater degree of balance. It also allows you to understand that most people's intentions toward you were not nearly as deliberate or malicious as they appeared formerly. In short, looking back allows you to become something of an observer in the past events you are examining. The positive aspect of being an observer of your own life, is that it is possible, as an observer, to see things in a more balanced and non-judgmental way. That same degree of objectivity makes it possible to take a fresh look at your own motives and actions and to possibly reassess your interactions with others. That in turn, could lead you to find less fault in others and perhaps, recognize your own in ways you've never been aware of. Therefore, not only growing and knowing yourself through the experience of reflection, but changing the way you react to other people and situations in the future.

As I have reflected on my own life, I have been surprised by the things these reflections have revealed to me. Many things that made no sense to me have come into new focus through this experience. As I continue to reflect on my past life, I see so many times that God was fashioning my path and this, in spite of the mistakes my free-will allowed me to make. I no longer question where I come from, how I got to this point, if I've done the things I was meant to do and if I need to fear the unknown?

I live these days of my life with less fear, more confidence, more compassion, less envy, more forgiveness and a much larger portion of love, joy and peace. All of this, in spite of the fact that I am still physically separated from my son. I feel his spirit with me nearly all of the time and that comforts me more than words can express, and yet, I miss him exceedingly, but not desperately. I am so grateful for the gifts God has given to me. I know I will see my son again and until that time; I live my life as a seeker of truth and enlightenment.

My son, Ethan, was a dedicated lover of music and to honor his memory when I write, I choose song titles to identify most of the chapters in my books. I only omit doing it when there is no song that comes to mind as I'm writing. My son's spirit communicates with me every day and often he will say, "Put some music on, Mom." I find myself doing that automatically these days and I find great comfort in both the music itself and the lyrics; it is a love Ethan and I still share.

When I began writing this book, I had written several poems and wanted to include them somewhere, in order to be able to share them with others. I wanted to have them relate to some of the other things I was writing. I knew I would need more poems than I had already written for this book and I expected that would be the hardest part; the poems came rapidly, sometimes every day. Sometimes, as soon as I laid down to go to sleep, I would hear the first few lines and know if I didn't get up and write it then, it would be gone. Sometimes the words came so fast, I was just scribbling to catch them all. I made very few alterations to the poems; they are presented almost in their entirety, the way I heard them in my mind. Some of them I'm really comfortable with and some not so much. There are a few instances, where I began to write my thoughts and suddenly realized I was writing thoughts that came from Ethan. Those are, of course, very special to me. I hope you enjoy the poetry; it seems to have stopped for now and I don't know whether to anticipate it's return in the future. Whatever will be, will be...

J.S. Schmidt

WHEN YOU WISH UPON A STAR

Starlight, starbright,
First star I see tonight
I wish I may
I wish I might
Have this wish I wish tonight!

If I could have anything I wished for, it would be to magically undo all of the hurt and damage that was done to my family, the day Ethan's life was taken. Even if in order to do so, I would have to bear everyone else's pain for the rest of my life. I would unbreak all of the hearts that were broken on that day. I would erase the painful intimacy all of my grandchildren have with death, so early in their lives. I would wipe away the anger from the hearts of my husband, my other two sons and perhaps, though it hasn't really surfaced yet, from the hearts of my grandsons. I would wave my magic wand and restore the love and companionship of my son to his grief-stricken wife. I would look into the eyes of everyone I love and see no traces of the pain that lingers there still.

Through the love of God, I have found my own place of peace, but sadly, I cannot share it with those I love with all my being. I have no magic wand to wave and make everything right again; I can only trust that God has a plan of restoration for each of them. I can only stand by, in hard won patience, as they mature and hopefully come to that point of peace that God is offering them. I can only encourage them to look in the right place to find it. It is so hard to know how far to go with them without overstepping the boundary of their own spiritual search. I have had 68 years to find my way to intimacy with God. They have had so little experience with spiritual things. At their age, I was still fearful and uncertain as to how safe it was to open some of those doors. I want to help them, but I don't want to frighten or even worse drive them away from a relationship with God.

I pray, I will be granted enough years with them that when the time comes for me to leave them, they will be spiritually mature enough to know that I have only gone to a new home, that is not so very far away from them. There is so much I would teach them, but I have to ask myself, *"Do I have the right to do so?"* Do I simply stand by and watch them struggle to find the way? I know, I can pray fervently that God, in His infinite wisdom and love will guide them. I hope, at least, I will have taught them to listen for His voice. I know from my own experience, that it can take a very long time to figure life out; many people never complete the task. Am I not myself a work in progress?

I am so deeply grateful and humbled by the work the Holy Spirit has done in my own life, since my heart was broken on that terrible day. He has filled my spirit with love and forgiveness, kindness and compassion, patience and peace. All of this, in spite of the loss of one who meant life itself to me. How can I share this miracle of God's love with them and make them understand its magnitude?

They have blessed my life more than there are words to describe and when I leave them, I hope they will feel how much I have loved them and will continue to love them and watch over them eternally. Spirits do not die and love that is true never dies. As long as they love me, I will always be with them. I hope they will remember my life as a blessing God gave to theirs.

A STAR IS BORN

On Saturday March 14, 2020, our family buried a much-loved young man of 51 yrs. of age; my husband's younger brother, Dan C. Schmidt. Many hearts were broken at his untimely and unexpected passing, from complications prior to a fairly routine surgery. On Sept.19, 2015 our family and friends gathered around us as we buried our son, Ethan, also a young man. A young man in perfect health who was taken from us by the act of another. These two tragedies for our family occurred almost exactly 5yrs. and 6 mos. apart. It felt way too soon to have lost either one of them; and way too soon to be experiencing such grief a second time.

If you have read my first book, you will know that I began to communicate with Ethan almost daily from the time he passed; many of those communications come through music. Last night, I experienced another wonderful, mystical communication from Ethan. Earlier in the day, I opened and read a card sent to us from our daughter-in-law Carol's parents; part of the personal message written in it said: "Dan and Ethan are together". I had no doubt that was true, but what I didn't know was if that had happened yet. I asked Ethan to show me a sign if Dan was with him. Three hours later, I heard it.

To give you a little background; in 2015 on what would have been Ethan's 40th birthday (Sept. 27th) my nephew Toby informed me that a major celestial event was going to take place, a "Blood or Red moon". A blood moon occurs approximately every two to four yrs. It is the last eclipse in a series of four eclipses that is known as a lunar tetrad. This one seemed very significant to me because of the recent loss of my son and it was to occur on his 40th birthday. The Bible speaks of a blood moon that will usher in the last days on earth, before the return of Christ; that also makes it a significant event, no one knows which blood moon that could be.

On the day of the red moon, we celebrated Ethan's birthday in the same way we always did and have done since his passing; we had beef and homemade noodles and angel food cake. We had some extended family and a few close friends with us that night. I witnessed the eclipse and the red moon for the first time that night; it was an unforgettable event.

So… after I asked Ethan to give me a sign about Dan, Tom and I sat down to unwind awhile before bedtime. I turned Pandora to my Enya station and turned down the lights, except for a small St. Patrick's Day tree that was lit up in the corner of the room. We were listening to some very soft piano and violin music and as that ended, a song began to play that I was unfamiliar with; I looked at my phone to catch the title and saw it was "Once Upon A Red Moon"! There was the sign I asked for; I have no other way to connect with a red moon except through the experience of seeing it on the night of Ethan's birthday, so close to his passing. The Bible speaks of many signs and wonders, but you must pay attention or you'll miss them: They must be seen and experienced with your spiritual senses.

I like to think that every star in the night sky is in memory of a spirit who lived for a time on earth and then departed. A new star was born when Dan passed the evening of March 10th. As with many other amazing spirits, Dan made the world a brighter place with his presence in it. The impact he had on so many lives simply can't be measured. That impact means the light that radiated from him here will never be completely extinguished; perhaps it won't shine as brightly, but the spark will live in the hearts of those who knew him and go on loving him. It will pass in some way to others who never had the opportunity to know him, because those that carry his light were changed by it in some way. There is no doubt in my mind that he gave some intangible thing to everyone that made them better; never worse or less than they were before they met him. His spirit of fun and his sense of humor and ability to always come back to a place of happiness, no matter what challenges he was dealing with, are an example of the light that fills his spirit. That spirit didn't die with his physical body; it has transcended worldly limitation and is now free. If he loved you that love will remain in your heart and a part of his spirit will always be with you.

As I sat in the service of celebration of Dan's life, I began to cry each time I looked at the picture of him on the stage; it seemed to be looking right back at me. Each time I started to cry; I heard him say "Suz, don't cry!" His spirit was there in that beautiful church; just as I knew it would be. I know we must grieve; we must shed our tears of love and loss, but he wants us to remember to seek our own place of happiness, when it is time to dry our tears and live with the new reality of his absence.

Whenever you look up at the night sky and see trillions of stars shining there, remember those you love who have gone to another place; do not remember with sadness, but with gratitude for having shared a portion of your life journey in their company.

Whatever you find to enjoy in your life; enjoy it a few seconds longer, for those you love who are now gone from this place. They live in you, and through you, until your own star shines in the heavens.

"Good Night, Sweet Prince;
And flights of angels;
Sing thee to thy rest."

Hamlet (Act 5, Scene 2, 351-2)

STILL OF THE NIGHT

In the still of the night;
When all has turned to black and white;
When shadows of gray come out to play;
And between the two shall ever stay.

When stars in the heavens their vigils keep;
When earth's weary actors have fallen asleep;
It's then come the spirits who hover above;
To visit the dear ones; those whom they love.

Sometimes, they appear in dreams as we sleep;
Sometimes, in a song or in memories we keep;
Always, they come in love and concern;
Someday, God's sweet mysteries we shall learn.

They loved us in life; they're loving us still;
They stay ever near and beside us until;
We reach the same portal all must walk through;
When the stars we shall see from a heavenly view.

Where the darkness of night; heaven's glory dispels;
Where breezes blow gently; midst the tinkling of bells;
Where all live in harmony, peaceful and blessed;
Where all who have labored, have found their sweet rest.

Where Jesus is waiting in a meadow so green;
Where waters run gently, sparkling and clean;
Where all you behold is bathed in sunlight;
Where all gray is forgotten, in heaven so bright.

J. S. Schmidt - Feb. 20,2019

IN MY REPLY

This chapter is a gathering of things I have written and then, through various means, have received a reply to. I won't be including every letter I receive in response to the letters I have written to Ethan since his passing; at this time, there are several hundred. I won't include the immensely personal replies I receive from Jesus when I write letters to Him. The response I have received and continue to receive from heaven has been so incredible and overwhelming; I couldn't possibly put all of it into words, but I can assure you these things have all occurred.

I am including a couple of poems I've written, that are followed by a reply from Ethan. In one instance, I thought I had finished the poem and suddenly there were more verses and instead of being addressed to Ethan, they were addressed to me, from Ethan.

The other poem is complete, as I wrote it and it was only when I read back through it, that I realized, it was him speaking to me.

These are such personal thoughts and feelings, but unless I share them, how will others know these blessings are possible. You don't look for things that you don't know exist as possibilities. My heart and soul know that I'm doing the things I'm supposed to do in order to help other people and help myself to live. I pray this sharing is a blessing to those who read my words.

This is a Facebook post, I left on the official page of the music group "Blackmore's Night" in June of 2018. This is another continuation of a story contained in my first book, LTBS. The chapter I'm referring to is titled, "The Village Lanterne". The following is the reply I received within about 24 hrs. of my post. This is what I wrote:

"I have wanted to tell you an amazing story about" The Village Lanterne *", for nearly three years now; I just wasn't sure how to do it.*

On Sept. 14, 2015, my youngest son, Ethan, was murdered as he sat in his office on the campus of Delta State University in Cleveland, Mississippi. I was shattered. Three days later, I was listening to music on Pandora and heard him speak to me through the songs that played. I know that sounds crazy, but it's still happening.

On April 27, 2016, just before Mother's Day, I received this message from Ethan: "I know Mother's Day is coming, and I know you'll be sad. You're still my mom and I still love you." Then, The Village Lanterne began to play. I didn't know anything about Blackmore's Night and I had no knowledge of that song. I began to cry immediately and when the song ended, I was sobbing and rivers of tears ran down my face. The rest of the message came after the song ended. "This is your Mother's Day gift from me. I knew you'd love this music! No more tears now, OK?

I just want you to know the power of what you do and how grateful I am for that song. Your music is so beautifully spiritual and comforts me more than I can say."

This was the reply I received from someone I understand to be Candace Knight, the author of the lyrics: *"Sending you so much love and healing. I am sorry about what you went through, but knowing that your son is still with you is such an incredible gift in itself. May the magic of the music continue to heal, strengthen and comfort you. Thank you for sharing your story with us."*

GIFTS

I held you in my arms that day;
Just minutes after birth;
That's when I gave my heart away;
For joy come down to earth.

You made my life, my family whole;
Your smile, it warmed my heart;
A precious loving baby soul;
I loved you from the start.

The years so quickly passed;
How wonderfully you grew;
We knew the time would come too fast;
When like a bird, you flew.

How proud we were as you became;
A man, a husband and father too;
A wife you took to share your name;
Then babies came; who looked like you.

Father and son came down the hill;
What a grand and glorious day;
It lives within my memory still;
How could it fade away?

My heart was broken on the day;
The worst of all my life;
When evil intent took you away;
And filled my world with strife.

I feel your love is with me yet;
Your voice I often hear;
Your loving touch I can't forget;
I sense you ever near.

When flowers beneath that stone I place;
I feel your hand in mine;
When I look into your smiling face;
I know you're living still, in heaven's light sublime.

God sent your spirit to my heart;
No evil's cruel intent;
Could keep us eternally apart;
Once earthly days are spent.

God still blesses through this grief;
He strengthens day by day;
His love a gift of sweet relief;
Can only take such pain away.

REPLY...

I love you forever;
Sweet mother of mine;
You are my gift;
From heaven divine.

Weep not my mother;
Let not bitter tears fall;
For I am still with you;
Whenever you call.

J.S. Schmidt and Ethan A. Schmidt

KINDRED SPIRIT

Kindred spirit, who knows my heart;
So full of sadness, to be apart;
The life we shared, now in the past;
The love we shared, will ever last.

I miss you so, each cloudless day;
I miss you still, when clouds are gray;
I feel your love, I know you are;
Sometimes so near, and yet so far.

How precious were the years we spent;
How fast they came and then they went;
Memories, like stars, fill the midnight sky;
I hold them so dear; they make me cry.

Don't live in the past, I hear you say;
Stay in the now, until the day;
The future is come, in golden light;
When eyes behold the longed-for sight.

REPLY...
When teardrops dim the light of day;
Let them fall without delay;
Let joy return to the grieving heart;
Begin again, a brand-new start.

My spirit sits beside you still;
You have my love, and so you will;
Till heaven and earth become as one;
And all is well beneath the sun.

J.S. Schmidt and Ethan A. Schmidt- July 5, 2018

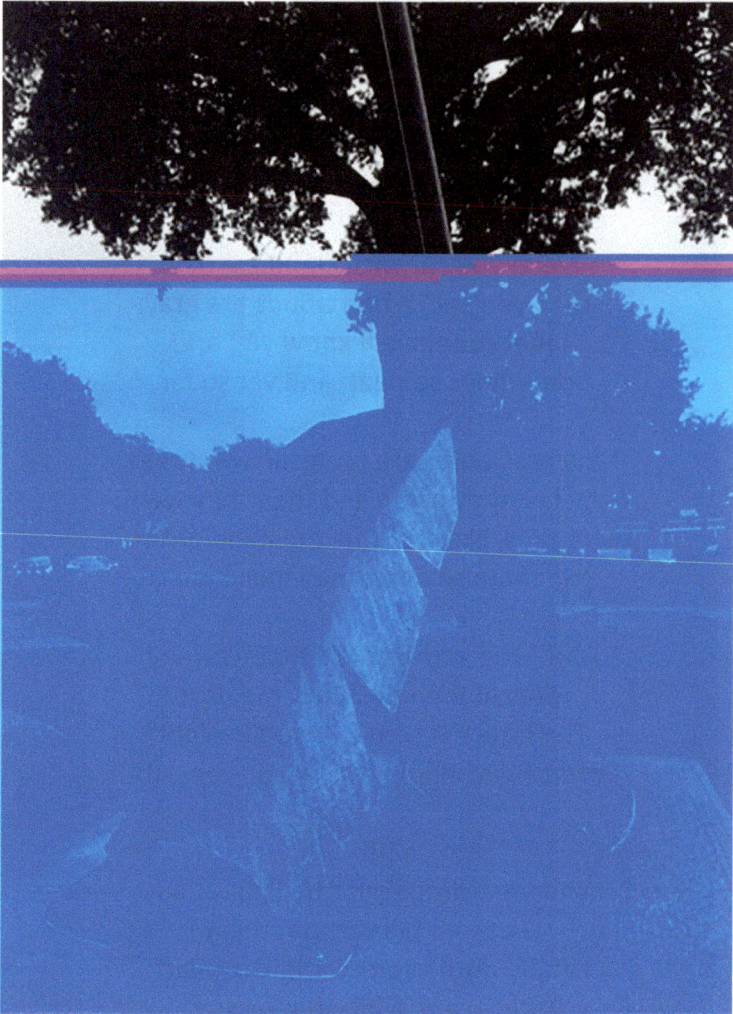

This metal sculpture, titled "Broken Arrow", was created in Ethan's honor, by artist Lawson King, a student at Delta State University. It is located at the Downtown Crosstie Trail in Cleveland, Mississippi.

IF EVER

If ever I should see you;
Standing near the shore;
Looking to the future;
Wishing there was more.

If ever I should find you;
Living in the past;
Sorting through the memories;
Of a life that didn't last.

If ever I should hear you;
Speaking of regret;
Knowing that it's useless;
But still you do it yet.

If ever I should touch you;
As you slumber in the night;
And fill your heart with gladness;
And ignite your spirit's light.

If ever I should say then;
Mom, you know it's really me;
Would it heal your wounded heart?
Would it set your spirit free?

If ever you should doubt;
That my love is living still;
I shall whisper to you softly;
And my words your soul shall fill.

If ever I should leave you;
And be truly gone away;
The stars would fall to earth;
From the distant Milky Way.

If ever in forever;
There are no words left to say;
You will know the end has come then;
For time has passed away.

If ever I should reach out;
And take you by the hand;
I will walk with you through heaven
Through God's Holy Promised Land.

August 12, 2019- Ethan A. Schmidt
Through J.S. Schmidt

ANGEL BAND

We live in a world that is inundated with images of angels; they are all around us. They can be found in pictures, figurines, on clothing, in jewelry and in statuary often found in cemeteries. In 2011, a CBS poll showed 8 in 10 Americans believe in angels; in spite of a poll by Pew Research Center that indicates less than 40% of Americans attend church regularly.

As a small child, I liked the thought of having a guardian angel. Even though I never sensed the presence of angels; I was sure they must be real. The Bible mentions angels 273 times in 34 separate books. I knew if the Bible talked about them as real beings, it must be so. As I grew older, I still believed in angels, but I never really relied on their presence in those inevitable situations of fear or danger or sickness that we all experience in our lives.

Several years before my son's life was taken, I began to wake up frequently during the night and sense something had been hovering over me. This happened numerous times and though it puzzled me, it didn't frighten me; it didn't feel like something threatening or ominous. I had the sensation that if I could just come fully awake a fraction of a second earlier, I would be able to see what was there; that never happened. I only began to understand this experience, in retrospect, after Ethan's passing.

In the first hours and days that followed the murder of my son, I was so emotionally and physically devastated I could barely stand on my own. If I was on my feet very long, I began to shake and my knees would go weak, so that if I didn't find a place to sit down quickly, I felt like I was in danger of falling. After a few days of this happening, I noticed that each time it occurred, it felt as if there was a person on each side of me, who seemed to be holding me up by supporting me in the area of my elbows. I can't remember exactly when it occurred to me that this invisible support was the work of angels. There are things that you know, though you have absolutely no proof. During this horrific time in my life, my eyes were opened to many spiritual truths. I began to remember the sensation of something that hovered over me at night and I realized that too was angels.

I felt the presence of these angel guardians walking beside me for many months, as though I could reach out and touch them. They gave me so much strength and courage, when I had none of my own. The sense of their presence has grown less distinct with time, but I never doubt they are there. I often pray before I go to sleep that they will stand beside me and guard and guide my dreams. After suffering a violent event, such as the one that took Ethan's life, there are many disturbing images that you fight to block from your mind while you are awake, but at night those images try to creep in while your guard is down.

I came to realize these angels have been with me all of my life, waiting in the background to be called into duty whenever needed. I often wish I knew their names. The angels mentioned in scripture have names, so I believe they all must have a name. Knowing they are watching as my life unfolds, gives me peace and a sense of security.

A few weeks after Ethan's passing, I decided to drive through the cemetery where his earthly remains are resting. I still lived in the town where the cemetery is located and even before losing my son, it was a place I frequently visited. I enjoyed the serene beauty and stillness there.

On this particular day, I was a few minutes early to pick up my sister from her job at the elementary school, so I was really just killing some time. As I crossed the highway and drove onto the brick road that leads to the black cemetery gates, I glanced up at the sky; there were numerous white fluffy clouds over the field next to the road. I was thrilled when I realized there were two very large cloud angels who appeared to be flying toward the cemetery. They were very detailed; one with long flowing hair and the other appeared to have a thick braid wrapped around her head. Even their gowns appeared beautifully draped and flowed from their bodies, then gradually thinned to wisps of cloud before fading into the blue sky.

In the early days of my grief, I spent a lot of time outside; it somehow seemed easier to breathe when I was out in nature. My attention was very often drawn to watching the clouds. I saw many "cloud angels" as well as feathers, doves and crosses. All of the gifts were comforting and reassured me that I was never alone in my grief; heaven was watching. I wanted to be able to show the angels to my sister, but by the time I picked her up they had disappeared. I still hold them in my memory. They were an amazing gift in that dark time for me. I still watch the clouds and look for angels there.

ANGELS

Angels hovering by my side;
Invisible and silent they do abide;
Though never seen and never heard;
I know they linger, no need for words.

One is on my left; one is on my right;
Their quiet strength;
They give me;
While keeping out of sight.

The truth at last my heart can see;
They've always been so close to me;
Walking so near through night and day;
Through month and year, they never stray.

Guardians sent from God's unfailing love;
On fluttering wing, they float just above;
When I in weariness find peace in sleep;
Watchful eyes, my soul at rest doth keep.

Safely am I kept from harm and every earthly care;
When I awake from deepest dreams, I always find them
there;
I slumber peacefully in gentle rest;
Beneath their gaze, content and blest.

J. S. Schmidt- Feb. 9, 2019

EARTH ANGEL

The angels I have previously written about were heavenly beings, but I believe there are angels dwelling on earth also. Perhaps, they are just ordinary people like you or me, but at times God gives them their wings, so to speak, and uses them to love, comfort and encourage someone who needs help. You may have been used by God for this purpose and are completely unaware that it was God who sent you to deliver encouragement to someone. You may think you simply had the thought to do it and did. Where do you believe those thoughts come from? God is love, so I believe every loving thought is from God; they are not our own and they are not there coincidentally. We as human beings get accustomed to believing that all of our thoughts are our own, not realizing that the Holy Spirit plants thoughts in your mind and heart. When you begin to hear more with your heart (heart thoughts), it becomes easier to recognize these "inspirational" thoughts as being God sent.

The most recognizable "earth angel" in my life, was a woman named Irene Pohlman. I met her about 40 years ago, when her son, Jim became the pastor at our church. From the moment I met her, I began to wonder if she was an angel. There are people who just seem to make the world a brighter, sunnier place and Irene seemed to bring light to any space she occupied. Perhaps, she was just so filled with the Holy Spirit, that she couldn't help but glow. When she smiled, which she did often, it lit her entire being; she radiated warmth. She was the happiest Christian I've ever known. My father, who was a lay minister for many years, used to say that many Christians give religion a bad name. I've also heard it said that many Christians look like they've been soaked in dill pickle juice. They have a very sour countenance. Christians are supposed to be the happiest people on earth. I've read that human beings are made of the same energy as the stars. When I think of Irene, it's easy for me to believe that's true. My memories of her are all happy and bright.

I remember particularly, the day of Ethan's celebration of life service; I can see her walking toward me as we greeted people before the service began. She was wearing a black dress and a beautiful smile. She hugged me and the first thing she said was, "You know he's safe now!" I did know that, and it was a relief. Then she said," He's a lot safer than we are!" I know she was as concerned about the state of the world as I am, but I also know she trusted in God's love to see us through whatever was to come. Surely, only an angel could radiate such warmth and light at a time of such darkness and pain, as that day was for me.

Irene loved angels; she had a huge collection of them in her apartment. I meant to go and see her angel collection when I had recovered my strength and balance, but I waited too long and her health began to fail. She had to move in with her other son who lived in another town; she was, after all, in her mid- 90's. Irene had suffered from a bad heart for many years, due to the fact that her body produced too much cholesterol. She was such a tiny, dainty little thing, you wouldn't have suspected she had that problem. She had to watch her diet very carefully. I find it interesting and slightly amusing that she was only allowed "Angel Food", if she wanted a piece of cake.

Irene always looked forward to Jesus' return; it turned out that she went to be with Him before He came back. I can only imagine how delighted she is to be with Him and His beautiful angels.

I attended the celebration service for Irene and I felt her spirit there in the church, so strongly. Just as happened with Ethan's spirit, I believe heaven let me know that she had arrived. As I made the 2-1/2 hr. drive back to my home on that day, the trees and the ditches seemed to be lined with red-tail hawks. There is a chapter in my first book that explains the special relationship I now have with red-tail hawks. I counted them on the way home because I was seeing so many, I was astonished. I counted over seventy that day and that doesn't account for the ones I saw before it occurred to me to count them. I have made that trip many times over the years and on a normal day I might see twenty hawks. I knew in my heart Irene was home with the Savior she had been anxiously waiting to see. Some people bring so much light into the world that when they leave, it becomes noticeably darker. I miss her illumination!

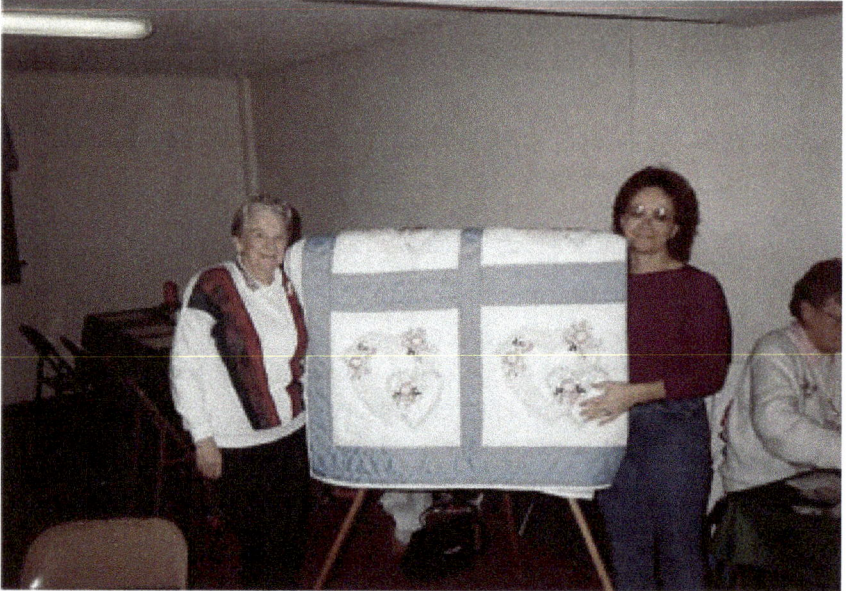

This is Irene Pohlman (on the left, the Earth Angel) and me, with a quilt made by ladies of our church as a fundraiser. I won the quilt and subsequently sold it to Irene's husband, because she wanted it so much that I couldn't resist making her happy. I donated the money to the church so we made money on the quilt twice.

COUNT YOUR BLESSINGS

Most of us don't spend nearly enough time focusing on the blessings in our lives. When we take the time to reflect on all that God has done for us, we usually only count the things we see as gifts; such as a good job, enough money, nice home, etc. Some of us go a level beyond that and include good health for ourselves and our families, the blessing of children, close friendships etc. Few of us pause to reflect on the blessings we received because something "didn't" happen.

Following the cataclysmic event of the murder of our son, I began to take a much deeper look at my life, both as it is now and as it was in the past. I realized there had been many times over the course of my then 64 years, that I failed to recognize blessings that happened and especially things that were blessings because they did not occur. You might be asking yourself how something can be recognized as a blessing, if it did not happen? Let me try to explain:

Most of my life I've had a tendency to try to anticipate what might happen in the future. I didn't like surprises and tended to see them almost entirely as negative. I tried to prepare for as many contingencies as possible. I've stopped doing that because it has been necessary for me to try to live in the moment, in order to maintain my balance, which was at first very shaky. Through Ethan's communications, the Holy Spirit has taught me that living in the "now" moment makes sense, because now is the only thing you can impact either in the positive or the negative. I have read that now is the only moment when heaven and earth intersect. Ethan also told me that trying to figure out what might happen (so I can prepare for it) is a waste of time and energy because you're going to be wrong more often than you'll be right. When I was in my early 20's, I was struggling with a failed marriage and I remember my now ex-husband telling me many times that everyone should *"just live for the moment."* What my brain heard every time he said that was, *"Right, everyone should ignore their marriage vows, their responsibilities such as debts, their job and their children."* I'm not trying to pick on my ex-husband here, I had my own issues and he's just mentioned here to make a point.

Now, I see there is a way to stay "in the moment" that does not include doing any of the above-mentioned things. As I wrestled with debilitating grief in the days, months and now years following Ethan's forced absence from my life, I came to understand that memories(the past) were initially very painful, but then I received a message, through Ethan, from the Holy Spirit that suggested I try to separate my memories from my pain. When I began to do that, it wasn't so painful to remember, but then, I began to try to live in the past to avoid the painful reality of the present and future. Ethan told me to enjoy my memories, but not to think it was realistic to try to live in the past.

I learned pretty early in the grieving process, not to look too far into the future. A future of indeterminate length, lived without my child was just too painful to contemplate. Ethan would remind me often to "stay in the now".

At some point, in spite of the loss we had suffered, I began to realize how many incredible things God was doing in my life. Those were current blessings and once I counted all of those and expressed my deep gratitude to Him for all He has done for me; I began to look back beyond my time of crisis and it was then I began to see clearly, all of the times God had stepped into my life to provide resources, protection, opportunity and strength and those are only a few of the numberless blessings God gave me, at so many points in my life, when I didn't deserve His love or His gifts. Every time I look back into the past, I have some new revelation of God's graciousness and love for me.

Blessings are not always something we ask for or something we think we want. Blessings are what God knows we need and wants to give us.

I realize now what an incredibly compassionate gift it was to Ethan and to me, that he didn't suffer and I didn't have to see him suffer. I know that many are not so fortunate in this regard and I don't know why it's necessary that anyone suffer at all; but God knows and I trust there's a reason.

Ethan didn't have to struggle to live a life in a severely disabled condition and I didn't have to stand by him, knowing there was nothing I could do to help him. I know many parents have had that horrific burden and my heart bleeds for them. I also know that had God chosen to allow us to experience that pain, He would have given us the strength and courage to bear it.

I think it's important to point out here that God gives you "enough" courage or strength etc., but only enough; there is none to spare; you make it through what you need to make it through and then you ask for more strength or courage or hope etc. to get over the next hurdle or walk the next mile. The key point is, *"ask and you will receive."* No matter what painful experience you or your loved ones are faced with, God wants to help you and He can help you in ways no mortal being can even contemplate.

God's Promises
God gives grace for each trial and courage for each sorrow
And faith to face in confidence a blessed, bright tomorrow.
Unknown

LATE AT NIGHT

When late at night, I sit alone;
And all have gone to sleep;
I listen to the songs we loved;
And I begin to weep.

For days so swiftly passed;
For moments held so dear;
For laughter, love and joy expressed;
When I kissed and held you near.

I try so hard to bravely stand;
The loss of one I've borne;
The tears still fall upon my cheeks;
My heart still beats forlorn.

I love you so and ever will;
Regret the time we've lost;
The memories of time we shared;
Now priceless at the cost.

Of peace and joy, my precious child;
Of golden years together spent;
Your hand in mine in quiet times;
Of cards you never sent.

Treasures I hold of life we knew;
In years of peace and love;
Blessings counted one by one;
Sent down from heaven above.

                                    J. S. Schmidt

DON'T BLAME TOLEDO

This is my second attempt at writing this chapter; the first draft just sounded very much like I WAS blaming Toledo and every other place that could have given Ethan a teaching position that would have gotten him out of Cleveland, Mississippi and nowhere near Shannon Lamb. I truly have forgiven Shannon for what he did. I don't believe he was a bad person; I hate what he did, but I don't hate him and I have every sympathy for what his family is going through to this day. I often pray for his soul and for those who love him. As hard as we struggle, I know it has to be even worse for them to reconcile what happened, with the person they know and love.

When you experience an unthinkable tragedy, it seems so natural to find a reason for it, that makes sense of it all. It seems natural to find a person, place or thing to assign the blame to. In my heart, I know that doesn't help, because it really doesn't change anything. Even if I could find the perfect place to assign the blame; Ethan would still be just as physically absent and I would still long to see him smile. I would still ache to see him standing at my front door. I would still be willing to give all I could ever have, to give his children one more day with him.

When I decided early on, I couldn't go on living with anger and bitterness in my heart, I knew I would have to try to find a way to forgive Shannon for taking Ethan's life. That meant there would be no assessing blame; I admit that requires a great deal of effort on an ongoing basis.

Getting back to Toledo; Ethan was somewhat conflicted about staying at Delta State for the duration of his teaching career. He loved his colleagues and the university in general, but being a transplant to the South, he struggled with the racial divisions that still exist there. I guess recently, it's become sadly obvious that they still exist in many places and in many hearts. Ethan received his PhD from Kansas University in Lawrence, Ks., which is a place of great diversity and he wanted his children to grow up being comfortable with all ethnicities; with that in mind, he decided to interview for positions at other schools. Sadly, he discovered that due to financial constraints, many universities were hiring adjuncts instead of PhDs. He interviewed at several institutions and felt really comfortable after his visit to Toledo. The search committee seemed very interested and he expected to receive an offer. When that didn't happen, he resigned himself to staying in Mississippi and continuing to work toward tenure, which would have come to fruition the year following the tragedy that ended his career and his life.

So, you see, Toledo stands out in my mind as a major disappointment. I bear Toledo nor anyone in it any animosity, just disappointment on behalf of Ethan and myself. I also bear no animosity toward Cleveland, Mississippi or Delta State University. Nonetheless, I could never go back there. It's hard to make people understand that it has nothing to do with the place itself; it is entirely about being too close to the horror that unfolded there. I can only bear it if I don't get too close. Had I been there at the time this tragedy occurred, I truly don't believe I could have survived it. The 500 miles between me and that moment in time barely saved me

I also have come to believe in my heart, though my mind doesn't want to agree, that Ethan's life was going to end at that time. If Shannon hadn't taken his life, I believe something else would have. It's painful to speculate about what that might have been, so I don't, but I also don't doubt that something was going to happen. Being able to see the truth is sometimes a two-edged sword. I see things and know things I would rather not know.

I try to focus, not on bitterness or blame, but on the immense gratitude I have that God sent me such a beautiful, happy spirit, who shared life with me, as my son, for nearly forty years. The hole in my heart reminds me just how big the space was that he occupied here.

I desperately want everyone who reads our story to understand that I speak of these things so near and dear to my heart, so painful to my spirit, not to point out that I am blessed in some special way to still have Ethan, in a spiritual sense, but to show that I believe this blessing can come to others who truly seek it. I don't know if I could even remember the exact path I followed or if it would lead someone else to the same place. I can't honestly say if I was led to this place or if I just stumbled on it as I staggered through my grief. I feel as if the point of my experience, after the event that precipitated my grief, is so that I can tell others these things are possible.

Forgiveness was never my strong suite, in fact, I rarely ever forgave anyone for any reason. I was very good at holding grudges; I could remember every little hurt or slight way back to my earliest years. I rarely ever gave anyone the chance to hurt me twice. It was almost 13 yrs. before I decided it wouldn't kill me to speak to my ex-husband; who I was sure had deliberately tried to ruin my life.

The word "decide" in the previous sentence, is crucial in discussing forgiveness. Forgiveness is a "decision" you make. You decide if you will forgive and when you will forgive; it's a deliberate choice. If you wait passively for forgiveness to imbed itself into your heart, you will never reach the point of peace. You will continue to live bearing the weight of bitterness and unforgiveness and it will impact the rest of your life. As Ethan has said to me, *"Unforgiveness and bitterness weigh down your soul and your spirit, and they should be soaring."*

If anyone had tried to tell me that someone was going to take my child's life and that in less than seven months, I was going to forgive them; I would have said: *"You're completely crazy. That isn't even possible."* Yet, that is exactly what happened. Without the Holy Spirit, it would never have happened. There is simply no other explanation. The only thing that changed was how I felt about what happened; my son is just as gone from my life here as he was on that awful day. Only God could have made forgiveness possible.

GRIEF

How many hearts have been broken?
How many tears have been shed?
When those painful words were spoken;
I'm so sorry, but he's dead.

Life and death lie hand in hand;
And loss, as surely as the wind;
Shall come to all, wherever we stand;
His peace and comfort God will send.

God will not leave us comfortless;
That comfort's ours, when once we ask;
The Spirit descends, our lives to bless;
But we must help complete the task.

If we reach out, God reaches too;
He takes the pieces broken apart;
And gives strength and peace to you;
If we but ask, He'll mend each heart.

Inside each heart, He leaves a space;
To hold the ones, you've loved and lost;
So, you may find them in that place;
Though life's final bridge they've crossed.

God will not leave you in despair;
When in anguished prayer you seek;
His love and comfort, you'll find Him there;
Though the future seems so bleak.

The road ahead you cannot see;
While darkness dims your sight;
But Jesus' love shall set you free;
As you walk within His Light.

Ask Him then, to hold your hand;
To walk you through each day;
Until at last in heaven you stand;
And grief has gone away.

J.S. Schmidt- July 13, 2019

THE PROMISE

What more can I say about grief that hasn't already been said? We all think we know what grief is, until it is suddenly upon us. Grief is like a mile high, 1000- mile wide brick wall. You can't go under it, over it or around it. Your body can't pass through it, but your **spirit can.** Painful as it is, that is the only way to reach the other side. You must endure what is yours alone to endure. Others can go with you, but your pain is not theirs and theirs isn't yours. Beyond this seemingly impenetrable wall there is peace. When we suffer immeasurable pain, we draw our limbs close to our body and curl up as small as we can or we become rigid and our breathing becomes shallow to steel ourselves against it. The pain of grief must be endured in openness, without restriction, and with deep breaths as though we are drinking in the comfort God sends to us. The true value of peace lies largely unrecognized. There is no physical substance on the earth that can even vaguely compare to it, not gold or diamonds or any other precious commodity.

Strangely, I could compare grief to natural childbirth; the nearly unbearable pain must be endured to find the pure joy at the end of it. No one can do it for you. They can hold your hand and try to sympathize, but in the end, you must do the work to receive the reward. Grief in this respect, is like redemption. Getting there can be painful, but to find the joy and peace of communion with God, you must go through times of struggle and pain; that is how we know we need God. It is how we grow; it is how we are transformed into God's precious jewels. As Annie Johnson Flint relays in her poem" God Hath Not Promised" We will not always have blue skies. There will be storms, there will be joys **and** sorrows. There won't be peace **without pain.**

None of us wants to suffer pain or loss or the sadness of grief. We all want calm waters; smooth sailing. We don't want to confront our own death. As much as we can, we look the other way and hope to go unnoticed by death and loss. We think if we don't talk about it, we can keep it from happening. These things come to us all at some point in our lives, regardless of what we do.

We are like young David, the shepherd boy, who stood before the giant Goliath with only a sling and a few stones; seldom do we show courage when we come face to face with our own death. David's courage wasn't his own; it was placed inside him by God. We can find our own courage and strength and the reward for standing bravely to confront such pain and loss, is joy and peace.

I have searched my own soul many times since my son's life was taken and never, have I found one shred of evidence that God willed that event to occur. I have come to believe that God cries with us in our grief. He does not require us to endure pain and loss as a sacrifice in order to receive the joy and peace He wants us to have. If God were as cruel as that, He would withhold His peace from our lives entirely. He could certainly do just that if He chose to, but I don't believe He denies peace to anyone who seeks it. I only know my own physical life would have ended, if when I sought His comfort, there had been no response. That response was amazing and overwhelming and it confirms to me His existence and His enduring love for all He creates.

When we observe the grief of others, it makes us anxious for them and we are willing to walk through hot coals barefoot, if they will just show us that they are all right. We do this in almost the same way we try to calm a relentlessly crying infant; we are willing to swing from the light fixture to bring their tears and discomfort to an end. Our task is not to depress grief as you would a bleeding arm, but to let the tears and grief flow freely without restraint, so they can cleanse the pain away. Our task is to sit by the one whose heart is broken, to hold their hand or hold them in our arms; as Jesus holds them in His. Our task is to listen, to have compassion and patience as they make their personal journey from darkness to emerge into the light once more. Words are not needed as much as an understanding ear; someone just to listen without judgment, who will not shy away from their pain and tears. We feel helpless in the face of another's grief, but we are not. With courage and compassion, which God will supply if we ask it of Him, we can give exactly what is needed in someone's darkest hours.

The 13th chapter of 1st Corinthians, The Love Chapter, says in part: Love is patient, love is kind. It always protects, always trusts, always hopes, always perseveres. Love never fails; and now these three, Faith, Hope and Love, but the greatest of these is Love. If we apply these words from the scriptures to soothing and comforting those we see in grief, we will fulfill Jesus commandment to us to love one another as He loves each of us.

We often remark about people, that they lack compassion; we say it as though it were an unchangeable fact. Compassion is a gift of the Holy Spirit; we can develop it just like we choose to develop any other God-given ability. It is ours for the asking and we should seek it.

Our lives in this world are bound to change in often unexpected and painful ways. We never know what a day will bring. This world is inconstant; thankfully God's love for us isn't.

JESUS, HOLD MY HAND

Speak to me, Lord;
For I don't understand;
Why the one that I love;
Was torn from my hand.

My mind won't accept;
What my eyes clearly see;
My heart is now broken;
He was taken from me.

The life I have known;
Is suddenly past;
Where has it gone;
Why didn't it last?

Hold me and keep me;
From falling apart;
I barely can stand;
With such pain in my heart.

Walk with me, Lord;
Give me your strength;
Through the rest of my life;
No matter its length.

Give me your peace;
Teach me to smile;
Show me the way;
I can walk one more mile.

The world is now darker;
I can't see the way;
Give my heart courage;
At the break of each day.

Help me to know;
I am never alone;
So much has now changed;
In the life I have known.

This isn't the end;
No, this can't be at all;
My grief must be spent
My tears they must fall.

Lord, hold my hand;
As each step I take;
I promise I'll try;
If just for Your sake.

I'll see the sun shine;
If I hold my belief;
I will come to the end;
Of this season of grief.

J.S. Schmidt- Mar. 15, 2020

I believe each of us has a part in ministering to the world. I also believe it is our choice whether to acknowledge or accept this gift. I wasn't aware of the part I could play, until I lost my son and sought God's help in order to find a way to go on. As I have begun to heal, through the love, inspiration and guidance of the Holy Spirit, I have come to recognize there is a part for me in the unfolding of God's plan for the world of time. You must realize none of these things have been my intention; or you will not recognize the Divine guidance in the things I want to share.

It was never my intention to share the story of my son's senseless murder, but I wrote and published a book, "Learn to be Still"; that documents, with intimacy, that painful experience. It was written initially in the hope that it would stand as a record of the events that occurred at that time, for my 5- year- old granddaughter.

My own grandmother lost her mother when she was five years old and I asked her once to tell me what she remembered about her, (my great-grandmother). There was almost nothing, except, that she loved to dance and her family considered it to be a character flaw. I found it very sad that she remembered so little about her own mother. I thought about my granddaughter and how close she and Ethan had been; having her forget him would be like losing him all over again.

As I worked on "Learn to be Still", the thought of publishing it began to slowly take shape. This happened, in spite of the fact, that I was initially opposed to sharing our story. There can't be anything more personal than losing your child. We were inundated with calls from news outlets that kept our phone ringing for about two weeks, following the event that took Ethan from us. I felt I had lost so much of him and I wanted to hold on tightly to what I had left. Telling the story of our loss to complete strangers was the last thing I was prepared to do.

The first book documents a trip to Washington D.C. to visit my sister's daughter, that took place about 6 months after Ethan's passing. It was at that time that I visited the National Cathedral and during a communion ceremony, recognized for the first time, that I was being led by the Spirit to *"take up my cross and follow Jesus."* That meant, in my heart and mind, that I was to begin to share in Jesus ministry of love and compassion, by helping other people in whatever way I could. I knew that was how God planned to help me recover from my own grief, by giving myself to this mission and in return receiving love and compassion.

I still didn't recognize or acknowledge this as a ministry. That didn't become clear to me until 1-1/2 yrs. later, when I had completed the manuscript for the book and began the process of publishing. I decided to try to self-publish for two reasons; the first was, that I felt much of the book had come to me from the Holy Spirit, speaking through Ethan, and I wanted it published with as few changes as possible. In addition to that, I didn't want it to be subject to acceptance or rejection, for reasons I couldn't impact. I knew it needed to be shared and I was determined to make that happen. It wasn't an easy process and there were times I wondered if we could succeed.

Over the years, I have been involved in ownership of three small businesses; a fabric shop, a floral shop and an antique/ flea market shop. As each of those businesses drew to a close, one thing stood out in my mind," *I don't like being in business!"*

As my husband and I began to explore self- publishing, it became clear that I would need to have a business license and sales tax number. Two months earlier, I had faithfully promised Tom that I would never be in business again. He had inadvertently been dragged into all of my entrepreneurial schemes. Once again, we went through the process of creating a business entity. One of the first questions to be answered was, *"what kind of business would it be?"*

Amazingly, the answer that popped into my head was, *"It's a ministry."* In all my years of constant thinking and planning, that thought had never occurred to me.

My father, his father and two of my great-grandfathers were all ministers and most likely the only thing they all agreed on, was that women weren't called to ministry. My father passed away three months after Ethan's life was taken, so there was no possibility of discussing this idea with him. At first, I thought, *"I can't do that, I don't want to dishonor my father's beliefs."* But, as I continued to think and pray about it, I began to have a deep sense of peace. I believe he's looking at things from a completely different perspective now and I feel I have his blessing.

When I began to think about what form this ministry would take, I knew the book would be a part of it. I hope I will continue to be inspired to write and there will be many more books to follow. As I write this second book, I have to admit having some of the same doubts that plagued me with the first one. I questioned what value it would have for other people. I expected a lot of negative feedback, over the otherworldly content of some of the material. Overwhelmingly, people reacted to it with positive emotion and many asked me to continue writing.

I remembered over the years, people who knew me, commented about my writing style, my love of telling stories and the fact that I talk a lot and speak rather loudly. When I rolled that into one thought, I came up with the idea of being a motivational speaker. It sounded more realistic to me than to call myself a preacher. I began to try to schedule speaking engagements with women's groups, mostly church women's groups. I guess you could say that's actually like preaching to the choir, but I thought it would be a good beginning. It has developed very slowly. I spoke publicly only three times the first year. I am awaiting further instructions from the Holy Spirit regarding that aspect of this new ministry.

Each time I speak about these experiences, I feel so blessed. Every time someone comes up to me after I speak and tells me I've given them hope or encouragement, or they tell me their own amazing story of grief and unexplained blessings, I know I am doing what I'm supposed to do.

I have discovered nearly everyone has a story to tell, but as I have said elsewhere, many are afraid to tell it. When you first begin to recognize blessings in the midst of grief it is both amazing and confusing. The paradox of feeling grief and gratitude simultaneously, creates an odd dynamic.

Telling other people about my experiences and learning of theirs has become another aspect of my "Rose of Sharon Ministry". I not only speak publicly, but I have had many private one-on- one opportunities to exchange stories with individuals eager to share their story of loss and grief. I chose the name, "Rose of Sharon", for a variety of reasons, of course, it is one of the adoring names given to Jesus. There is also a very old hymn called, "Jesus, Rose of Sharon". It was written in 1922 by Ida A. Guirey. It's taken from the "Song of Solomon". In it, the Shulamite maiden who is to be his bride speaks these words to Solomon: *I am the rose of Sharon, and the lily of the valleys."* Jesus, though often referred to as the Bridegroom, is also described as beautiful and perfect; like an exquisite rose. Sharon, is a plain in Palestine where many beautiful flowers grow. The song, "Jesus, Rose of Sharon", was one of my father's favorite hymns and he often made me promise to have that song played during his funeral service. Using that name for my ministry is a fond remembrance of him as well. As I have previously mentioned, I used to own a floral shop and I discovered a deep love of roses. Every time I put them in a bouquet or arrangement, I marveled at their perfect symmetry and incredible scent. I know such beauty as this isn't accidental; only God can create such beauty and perfection and do it repeatedly.

THE CROSS

There stands a Cross;
In the darkness of grief;
Lifting me up;
Bringing relief.

There stands a Cross;
Giving its light;
Calming the storm;
In the darkness of night.

There stands a Cross;
Destroying my fear;
Holding my hand;
Drying each tear.

There stands a Cross;
Jesus is near;
His comforting words;
Through the darkness I hear.

There stands a Cross;
I reach out my hand;
Dawn's light is breaking;
Grief's torturous band.

There stands a Cross;
Where always it's been;
Waiting to heal;
And help me again.

There stands a Cross;
When all else departs;
Bringing me love;
Renewing my heart.
   J.S. Schmidt-Sept. 12, 2017

HOPE

Hope lives in the darkest of days;
Steadfastly, remains, in a million little ways;
In deepest despair, hope is still present there.
It lives deep inside for the Spirit to share.

Once, I believed my hope was destroyed;
By the evil one's tool; the one he employed;
Who had stolen the life of one that I cherished;
Who first, I believed, from this life had perished.

The evil one tried to deceive and to take me;
But, the Lord held me fast and refused to forsake me.
God's flame in my soul, refused to go out;
His strength and compassion rose up all about.

Hope lives in the soul, it lives in the heart;
It can't be destroyed, by the one set apart;
From all that is Holy and loving and sure;
The Rock, the Redeemer, beloved and pure.

In Jesus, my hope, my faith and my peace;
Imbues me with strength, until life here shall cease;
Till He stands just beyond the heavenly door;
And I run to His arms, to be safe evermore.

J.S. Schmidt-May 16, 2019

THE LIST

As I faced the rest of my life; my new life, without my son, I had no idea how to begin to create that life. I didn't realize that God already had a plan. I felt so empty and unfocused on that first Monday morning as I strolled through my backyard, alone for the first time since I received the phone call that stopped the life I had known for 64 years, in its tracks.

Tom left that morning with Ethan's family to drive them back to Mississippi. He was going to stay as long as it took to help Liz handle the necessary business details that needed to be addressed right away; things like life insurance, Ethan's retirement fund, etc. He was gone about ten days and other than the time I spent with my sister Jeanne; I was mostly alone. I knew it was necessary for me to spend some time on my own, in order to find my balance and try to focus, but it was also something I was uncertain about doing. I was afraid of thinking about what had just happened to my son, I was afraid of thinking about the past that had been so good and now seemed destroyed, I was afraid to contemplate the future because I thought it must most certainly be empty, painful and bleak.

I knew God would help me, but I didn't know how or where that help would manifest itself. I had a lot of time to think and that was both good and bad, intermittently. I knew God would expect me to at least try to help create the life I would lead going forward.

During that time alone, I decided to make a "Comfort List". The idea was loosely based on the so-called "Bucket List". If you happen to be unfamiliar with that term, it relates to a list that terminally ill people sometimes make; sort of a last to-do list that encompasses things they want to do that they just never got around to doing for various reasons.

My "Comfort List", was comprised of things I believed would help me regain my balance and calm my bewildered spirit. I won't go into everything that was on my list, but I think some of those things are relevant to talk about in this book. There were 18 items on the original list. At this point in time, I have completed 10 of those goals. Some of them were ridiculously easy, some depended on the cooperation of other people and some took me really far out of my comfort zone.

The first item on the list, (they were in no particular order, I just wrote them as they came to me.) was to buy myself a new Bible. I had never owned my own Bible, I just used whatever happened to be around the house. I've always been partial to the King James translation, (originally published in 1611) because I love the sound of words and much of it is beautiful when read aloud. I understand it's harder to study from, but I was doing my best to stick to those things that were most familiar, in the midst of the chaos that followed our personal tragedy.

I bought a new KJV Bible and within a few weeks had read the entire New Testament. I had read most of it before, but never from beginning to end. When I began to feel the Holy Spirit urging me to share the story I was now living, I began studying the Bible with renewed interest. I realized that suddenly, many old familiar scriptures seemed brand new and their meanings had such simplicity and clarity.

As I look back nearly four years later, I realize it was the Holy Spirit that prompted me to include purchasing a new Bible. How often we fail to recognize the Spirit when He (She) is working so diligently to change our lives.

In the first book I wrote," Learn to Be Still", I mentioned the minister who co-officiated at Ethan's service; his name is James Pohlman, Jr. I know him as Jim. He is an odd mix of gruffness and tenderheartedness. You have to know him well to gain an appreciation for the juxtaposition of those two aspects of his personality. Jim was one of the first people to arrive at my home to offer his help and to pray with and for me.

As a long -time minister, he has been an inside observer and inadvertent participant in innumerable scenes of grief and tragedy. He cries easily and loves deeply. Perhaps, it is his gruff side that allows him to offer himself up to these most painful moments in the lives of others and not be destroyed by them.

Jim is a Navy veteran and a former police department canine officer. That's where the gruff side of his personality likely comes from. There is not an ounce of pretension in him, he is as he is, without apology. Getting back to his softer side, and how he made the list: He plays piano beautifully and with a sort of personalized, but classic style. I've always loved to hear him play, which he occasionally did during worship service at the church we attended for over twenty years. Item number 8 on my list was, "listen to Jim Pohlman play hymns on the piano." I called him one day and asked if he would meet me at the church, at his convenience, and just play whatever he wanted to play. He was willing, though he said he hadn't been playing much in recent years and was a bit rusty. He brought his wife, Sara, with him and we sat together in the front pew and listened as he played whatever hymn I selected and all from memory. Sara was suffering from a form of dementia and Jim no longer left her home alone; I was glad she was there that day.

Less than two years later, Jim lost his mother, Irene, and then Sara, within 4 months of each other. It was a terrible blow to lose the two most important women in his life, in such a short span of time. I wish we could have been there for him in his time of grief, as he was for us. We no longer live in that community, so that hasn't been possible. I send him a card every now and then, just to let him know we think of him. Life happens to us all and death is a part of life. Our lives are connected so much more deeply than we realize and as Ethan so often reminds me; In the end there is only love.

THE COMFORT LIST

1. Buy myself a new Bible
2. Go to the zoo and watch the otters swim
3. Go to Botannica (Wichita, Ks.)
4. Have supper with my friend, Trina
5. Begin writing in a journal
6. Buy art supplies and learn to paint sunsets
7. Finish the quilt I was making for Ethan and Liz
8. Listen to my friend Shane play gypsy jazz
9. Listen to Jim Pohlman play the piano
10. Visit the Arboretum at Belle Plaine, Ks.
11. Read poetry
12. Write poetry
13. Have a "vintage" movie marathon
14. Visit Leyla (my niece) in Washington D.C.
15. Take my grandchildren to Disney World
16. Visit Prague
17. Visit Tom's Uncle and Aunt in Ohio
18. Visit New Orleans

DIARY

Sometimes, I am in the mood to view life in the purest and simplest terms. At times like this, I very often make a statement like; there are two kinds of people...The majority of the time I don't see life in such black and white terms. I'm much more fascinated by the infinite tones, shades and hues life presents. Forrest Gump's mother told him "Life is like a box of chocolates," and so it is, but it is also like a box of Crayola Crayons. There are blues in light, medium and dark shades. There are blue-greens, blue-violets, blue-grays etc. The colors of life are infinite. I have also made this rather blunt statement at times: There are two kinds of people...there are numbers people and words people.

I am unquestionably a words person; I've always loved words. I love the way they sound, especially when read aloud. I love the way they look on a page. I love them handwritten or typed. I love the various meanings they convey and the emotions they evoke. I especially love the rhythm they create.

When I was in high school, I took a creative writing class and was amazed at how it made my spirit soar. I always thought someday I would try to write a book. My intention was to write fiction and perhaps, one day I will. I never dreamed I would write about losing my child or anything that was so personal and painful.

I didn't write often during the years I was struggling with a bad marriage and divorce. When I remarried and spent the next twenty years raising my children, I seldom wrote. Occasionally I would write poetry, but only when in a heightened emotional state; such as following the death of a family member or close friend.

Journaling was one of the things I included on my "Comfort List". It was actually my husband who suggested I begin to document all of the amazing things we began to experience during the painful aftermath of losing our son; much of what I wrote became my first book "Learn to Be Still". This book also includes some things from those early journals.

I often suggest to people who are grieving, that the simple act of writing their thoughts might help them move forward. The reply I get most often is *Oh, no, I'm not a writer!* The fact is that you are not writing a novel or anything like that; you are only documenting your own thoughts on paper.

I found journaling to be so helpful to me during that painful time, that I began to keep numerous journals, simultaneously. I began a" prayer journal" because my thoughts were so fragmented at that time that I couldn't even pray without losing my focus and my mind would wander. It seemed so disrespectful, so I began writing my prayers; I soon found they were so much more cohesive and comprehensive. It was so much easier to remember to pray for other people when I was writing their names in my prayer journal. After about two years, I thought I could stop writing my prayers, but I realized that even though my thoughts had become more organized as time passed, I still did a better job of covering everything I needed and wanted to say if I wrote it on paper. Recently, I have begun to realize that I pray intermittently throughout every day and so don't feel the need to have a set time of prayer.

In writing my first book, I discovered that for me there is a big loss of creative flow if I skip the step of physically writing my thoughts with my favorite pen on paper. At one time, I thought it made more sense to skip that step and just write while sitting at the computer, it just doesn't work for me to do it that way. It somehow feels so much less personal and it dulls the emotional aspect of what I'm trying to relate.

At about the same time I began writing in my first journal; which was kind of a way to track my thoughts on any given day; I read about something called an "Angel Catcher". It is a journal created by Kathy Eldon and her daughter Amy, following the murder of her son Dan Eldon. He was a 22yr. old photographer for the Reuters news agency. While on assignment in Africa he was stoned to death by an angry mob (1993). The Angel Catcher is designed to preserve memories, impressions and stories of the loved one who's gone from your earthly life. It contains prompts that are designed to help the grief-stricken begin to record their feelings of loss, sadness, anger, and frustration, as well as stories of better times spent with the one you love and lost; there is even an envelope pocket at the back to hold special messages or mementos; in the pocket of my Angel Catcher is the birthday card I intended to send to Ethan for his 40th birthday, which would have been two weeks after his passing; it was laying on my dining room table on the day his life was taken.

I purchased an Angel Catcher for myself and wrote in it my most personal and intense thoughts about what I was experiencing in those first months of grief. There were times I simply wanted to say 'Good Morning, Ethan. I love you!" Of all the things I have written since Ethan's precious life was taken, the things contained in my Angel Catcher reveal with intimacy the raw despair and devastation I experienced in that time. Those words, written nearly four years ago are so hard for me to read now. The" Angel Catcher" helped move me toward a desire to go on living my life, even if it was a different life than the one that had been stolen from me.

If you are struggling with your own grief, I highly recommend you try to get some of your own thoughts and feelings down on paper. They will still belong to you and you never have to share them with another soul, if you choose not to. For myself, it has been a great relief to be able to put them on paper and walk away from them, even if only for a little while.

SUNRISE, SUNSET

On the day we returned home from Mississippi, we traveled the same road as the hearse that was carrying Ethan's earthly body home to Kansas. There were many thoughts and memories of him running through my mind during that long and painful trip to bring him home for the last time to rest in beautiful Prairie Lawn Cemetery, just outside Peabody, Ks.

Earlier that day, as I rode in Ethan's van, with Tom driving and Ethan's oldest son Connor riding in the passenger seat in front of me, I experienced one of the first of several miracles God has blessed me with. I heard Ethan speak to me; though he had passed from this life three days prior to that moment, when I heard his words telepathically. Up to that moment in time, I had no idea that such a thing was even possible. It is nearly impossible to describe that moment or what it has meant for my life and recovery from deepest grief. I suddenly turned a corner I didn't even know existed and which I did not see coming. The hysteria that had been my companion for those three torturous days, left me. There was suddenly a peace in my heart that came from outside this world. I felt calm, and warmth radiated from the heart I believed was broken beyond repair.

Around 6-7 pm, we crossed over into Kansas from Oklahoma. The sun was setting; the most amazing and unusual sunset I ever remember seeing. I've tried so hard since then to find the right words to describe it and I'm still searching. I see it pretty clearly in my mind's eye, even now, nearly four years later. I began to think perhaps, I should try to paint it. I have very limited artistic ability, so I'm not at all sure I could do it justice. I only know the need to express the beauty of that experience is still with me.

Number 6 on my 'Comfort list" was to buy some art supplies and learn to paint sunsets." I actually bought the supplies, but have never attempted to recreate what I saw that day. Perhaps, that will happen sometime in the future.

The rising and setting of the sun has become much more significant in my life, as I have walked the road from grief to recovery. I often think how disappointing it must be to the Creator, to have produced something so breathtakingly beautiful and to recreate it every day, only to have it largely ignored by those you gave it to.

On the morning of the service that celebrated Ethan's life, Tom and I got up early and sat on the back porch of our home together, hand in hand, and waited for the sun to rise. We sat on the same porch Ethan sat on only a few weeks earlier, as he watched me water patio flowers and my flower gardens. He was in a pensive mood that day and he told me how much he loved coming "home", and having all of his family around him. He told me how much he loved returning to his hometown, that held so many happy memories for him.

Ethan loved so many things about life and that included music, art, and theater, to name a few. He performed in numerous plays and musicals, both in high school and community theater. One of those productions was "Fiddler on the Roof". The title of this chapter is also the title of one of the well-known songs from that musical. Whenever I remember that incredible sunset, I observed on the day we brought Ethan home, I think of that beautiful song. He was so happy to be in a production that included his cousins, Leyla and Toby.

Ethan was fortunate enough to be chosen for several supporting roles in high school. He was okay with being in a supporting role, but the role he most wanted to play was

King Arthur in the musical Camelot. He was so excited when he came home and told me the role was his. He asked me to make his costume, which I was happy to do. He really liked it and we had one of his Senior pictures taken in it.

When people tell me they've never heard God's voice, I always think to myself, *"Yes, you have; God speaks to you every morning when the sun rises and every evening when the sun sets below the earth's horizon.* God has many ways of speaking, other than in an audible voice.

The sunrise is a symbol of awakenings; it most obviously represents awakening from sleep or rest. It can also represent spiritual awakening. It can represent renewal or beginning again. It can represent emerging from darkness (physical, emotional or spiritual emergence).
The sunrise represents the gift of another day of life, another chance to try to get it right, to try to understand, to try to remember why you're here. It represents hope.

Sunset represents culmination, it beckons us to take our time of rest. Rest is the renewal of the mind, body and spirit. Sunset isn't a symbol of the end of something, it's really just a pause, because it is always followed by a period of quiet rest and then the glorious sunrise.

I realized as I grew more appreciative of the gift God gave us in these two wondrous events that reappear each day, I had spent most of my life short-changing their magnificence. What I mean is; I would rarely get up early enough to watch the actual rising of the sun, and if I did, I often missed the earliest part of this beautiful phenomenon. If you start to observe it before the first rays of light streak the darkened sky, you realize a lovely anticipation that builds, as you see the horizon subtly change from darkness to dawning and beyond to complete illumination. If you start too late or stop watching before it's fully bloomed, you miss the thrill of that anticipation that turns to complete recognition of the wonder of God's universe and His amazing gifts to us.

I discovered I had been short-changing myself in exactly the same way, in my observation of the sunset. I often would go for a short drive into the countryside, where I could have a more unobstructed view, but many times, I would arrive after the sun was already sinking behind the horizon. I would watch until I could no longer see any part of that molten red or pink ball and the sky was a pale shade of lavender and then I would begin my short drive back into town. I began to notice that often the prettiest colors emerged after the sun was completely set. I realized I had missed so many wonderful experiences of beauty, because I was trying to pin it down to my own timing. God does incredible things, but always, in His own divine right time.

If I think of the sunrise or sunset in a purely spiritual way, I can see that just as God's most precious gifts are given to us at times when our happiness and peace is obscured by the storm clouds of life; the sunrise and sunset are most magnificent when there are clouds present. Clear skies leave nothing for the sun's rays to penetrate or rebound off of, cheating the observer of a more colorful experience.

Every life will experience dark or cloudy days, but behind the clouds the sun is still shining; just as God's light still shines when our lives are obscured by the darkness of grief and loss.

Keep your faith in all beautiful things.
In the sun when it is hidden,
In the Spring when it is gone.

Roy Rolfe Gilson

Ethan as King Arthur in the musical "Camelot".

THE PAINTER

I awoke today;
Not far away;
From the home I used to know.

My memories sweet;
Lay strewn at my feet;
Bathed in heavenly glow.

I strolled the ground;
And there all around;
Rose joy, love and beauty to see.

In the dancing mist;
In radiance kist;
An arbor stood before me.

And there I found;
With ribbons bound;
Canvas, pencils, paint and brushes.

A bluebird sings;
As he happily swings;
On boughs of greenest branches.

In peace and pleasure;
No earthly measure;
Could ever know or tell;

I sit in fragrant bowers;
And pass the timeless hours;
Joyfully painting the angels faces.

J.S. Schmidt

In Memory of
Dorthea A. Strotkamp

Dorthea (Dot) Strotkamp was my sister's mother-in-law, an artist and a loving mother and grandmother. In fact, she was in many ways a bonus grandmother to my own children, as well. I will forever remember the softness of her manner and the gentleness of her spirit.

CITY OF NEW ORLEANS

When I began to hear Ethan speak to me through song lyrics, I noticed certain patterns developing. One such pattern involved songs that in one way or another brought thoughts of New Orleans. Ethan visited New Orleans on at least three occasions; it was a place he really connected to. As he began to communicate through music, there were several songs that played with notable frequency, that spoke to me in some way of New Orleans. These are the songs I remember hearing:

"House of the Rising Sun"
"Listen to the Music"
"City of New Orleans"
"Dance with Me"
"Ramblin' Man"
"Black Water"
"Born on the Bayou"
"Like A Rolling Stone"

Some of the songs mention New Orleans in the title and some mention the city in the lyrics. I am unable to quote song lyrics due to copyright laws, but if you are interested, you can listen to the songs on YouTube. I will try to briefly explain the significance these songs had for me in the context of Ethan's messages.

House of the Rising Sun is about a brothel in New Orleans, so this one is an obvious reference to the city.

Listen to the Music is a song by the Doobie Brothers, that was recorded in a studio on Toulouse Street, in the French Quarter of New Orleans.

City of New Orleans is about a train by that name. It was written by Steve Goodman and recorded by Arlo Guthrie

Dance with Me is a song recorded by the group Orleans.

Ramblin" Man is a song recorded by the Allman Brothers Band and there is a reference to a trip to New Orleans in the lyrics.

Like A Rolling Stone is a song written and sung by Bob Dylan. I kept hearing it mixed in with all of these other songs about New Orleans, but it didn't seem to have an obvious link to the other songs, until I discovered that it's on the "Highway 61" album and Highway 61 originates in New Orleans and ends in Wyoming, Minnesota, not far from Bob Dylan's home in Hibbing, Minn.

Black Water is another song by the Doobie Brothers. It doesn't have a direct reference to New Orleans, but it mentions Dixieland music and the Mississippi River which ends in New Orleans, as it flows into the Gulf of Mexico. It also mentions streetcars which are used as a form of public transportation there.

Born on the Bayou is a song recorded by Creedence Clearwater Revival that mentions New Orleans and Cajun queens.

As I started to hear the songs repeatedly, I began to think of the connection between them and realize there were times I was hearing them strung together consecutively. There were times I would hear 3 or 4 of these songs back to back and on at least one occasion, I heard 5 of the 8 songs in one listening session. They were making an ever-increasing impression in my mind and I began to sense that Ethan wanted me to go to New Orleans. That might not seem significant to you, but that was a thought I had never had independently and in fact, it was a place I really had no interest in going, prior to this time.

My husband and I don't travel a lot and when we do it's almost exclusively to visit family; none of whom have ever lived in New Orleans. Tom wasn't the least bit interested in going there with me and I seriously doubted he would agree to my going alone. I was right about that, but he suggested, if I could get my sister to go with me, he'd be happy to pay for the trip. That in itself is strange, because before the tragedy that took Ethan from us, Tom would never have thought it was okay for me to travel to an unfamiliar location without him.

It was 2-1/2 yrs. after Ethan's passing and many delays later that Jeanne (my sister) and I boarded a plane in Kansas City, bound for New Orleans. During those intervening days and months, I tried hard to figure out why Ethan would want me to go there. Was I supposed to see something significant? Or meet someone or was I just going to sense something spiritually? He just kept telling me to go there, so I had no real thoughts as to what I was supposed to do, once I got there. As I looked back through the journals I began keeping shortly after Ethan's passing, I saw that the sense that Ethan wanted me to take this trip began to form pretty quickly; it was about 6 months after his passing. New Orleans is considered by many to be a very spiritual location, so I began to focus on that thought. One thing that was included in nearly every brochure I saw, was the cemeteries. I thought perhaps that might be a place where something would trigger the revelation, I believed was the reason for making the trip.

Jeanne and I decided to spend our first full day in New Orleans on the city tour bus, which picked us up at our hotel. We planned to strike out on our own and possibly revisit anything we hadn't had time to fully explore the first day, on day two.

The city bus tour took us to one of the largest cemeteries and we had about 15 minutes to walk around. The cemeteries there have a very distinctive appearance; all of the graves are above ground in cement mortuary buildings or in walled graves, built on the edges of the property. Some of the tombs were very beautiful with large urns filled with flowers and statuary depicting angels etc. Sadly, there was a tremendous amount of damage there, due to the many hurricanes that have flooded the city over the years. Our time was limited there and it wasn't possible to do much exploring. I didn't get any particular spiritual feelings there, so I decided that wasn't the point of the trip. Our tour continued through the Cajun and Creole neighborhoods, which also were still badly damaged from Hurricane Katrina, which much to my dismay, hit New Orleans on my birthday, August 29, (2005)

The next day we caught a street car a few blocks away from our hotel and went to the French Quarter. I thought perhaps, I might discover something on Toulouse Street (Listen to The Music); again, there was nothing notable. We visited the St. Louis Cathedral and while it is a beautiful building, I felt no particular sense of anything connected to it. We sat by the Mississippi River and watched the paddle wheelers and the barges and looked out into the Gulf of Mexico, but I didn't feel anything special. All in all, it was a very enjoyable trip and a much-needed diversion from the grief that pervaded my life every day, but I began to think I had been mistaken as to the spiritual significance of it. When I returned home, I received this message from Ethan:

"New Orleans is such a melting pot of cultures and it offers a different vignette of the South and the stereotypes associated with it. There really is a deep spirituality living beneath the surface of what seems to be abandonment and debauchery, that was born of struggle, loss and change (the same things you've experienced with grief). It is a place of great faith in the future and reverence for the past. It has survived trials of epic proportions and still it

rings with laughter and music. If a place could become human, New Orleans would be the most incredibly talented musician and he would play amazing blues, jazz and zydeco and a combination of all three."

I believe the New Orleans trip was meant to demonstrate that not only can we survive the greatest tragedy; we can live with joy, laughter and a happy spirit. It was a wonderful gift!

Visiting New Orleans was #18 on my Comfort List!

JOY

Joy once lived, and then was lost;
Tragedy and pain the cost.
Where once it lived, within my heart;
I locked it there, now set apart.

I counted joy, but one more loss;
But faith still lived, beneath a cross.
A healing warmth, inside me grew;
The light of love, my life made new.

A voice I knew, I heard once more;
Bringing truth, peace to restore.
In disbelief, my spirits rose;
To heights unknown; a path disclosed.

The path I walked away from pain;
Has led me where Love's peace, I gain.
Within my heart, my joy now found;
Living still, has been unbound.

J.S. Schmidt- Nov. 21, 2018

SPIRITS

How precious is life;
Unique is each spirit;
The song of each heart;
When we're privileged to hear it.

Each spirit united;
As links in a chain;
As the sand on a beach;
Or as droplets of rain.

Spirit of heaven;
Into each child is born;
Its memories erased;
As the darkness at morn.

They arrive here so helpless;
So fragile and small;
So dependent on others;
To help them stand tall.

Three spirits God gave me;
To answer my prayer;
Each one so beloved;
To handle with care.

One spirit so sweet;
The next spirit strong;
The last one so happy;
Each sang their own song.

Each spirit that comes here;
Comes from God's heart;
They come with a destiny;
A time to depart.

They belong to the Father;
It's to Him they return;
He loaned them to me;
So, my heart's love could burn.

How sad was the parting;
Of the one who returned;
To the Father in heaven;
Each lesson well learned.

We love him and miss him;
And we long for him here;
For our circle was broken;
When we lost one so dear.

He waits at the end;
Of God's rainbow so bright;
To welcome us home;
At the end of our flight.

How grateful I am;
For each moment we spent;
With that bright, happy spirit;
Who from heaven God sent.

J.S. Schmidt-April 14,2019

My three sons, Left: Brett, Right: Jeff, standing: Ethan.

SUPPERTIME

We all have moments when a word or a song, an aroma, or anything else that awakens your senses, can transport us back to another time and place or event and a memory is triggered. It's not exactly a "déjà vu" moment, but a memory you have that may not have surfaced in such a long time, you are a little surprised to realize it's still there. I have a lot of memories like that which have come to the forefront, since I no longer have a physical relationship with Ethan in this world. Many of these memories are pretty mundane, everyday things; just the business of life, you might say. For instance:

I was mainly a stay at home Mom. I worked away from home on occasion, but only if it worked with the hours the kids were at school. We didn't want our children to be in daycare and as long as we could manage financially, that was the choice we made. So, since I was home nearly every day, I cooked a meal every day that was usually ready to serve by 6pm. That was the time we could all sit down together for "Supper".

My oldest granddaughter and I have a running disagreement about how meals should be identified. At my house, we have breakfast, dinner and supper. In her home they have breakfast, lunch and dinner. After much discussion, I told her I thought we should just agree to disagree and that whatever your mother called it was what you would probably call it also. No matter whether you call it dinner or supper, it's always been a special time of day for me. I looked forward to everyone who had gone off in the morning to work or school, coming home safe and sound; it gave me a sense of inner peace. I felt like the mother hen in the story books who gathered all of her little chicks under her wings at dusk and kept them safe and warm. I am also one of those people who believes feeding people is a way of nurturing them and showing them love. Those evenings we spent together in our home as a family of five provided a wealth of pleasant, peaceful memories for me. When we are busy raising our children, it seems like it will go on that way forever, but it comes to an abrupt end one day; the day that last little chick has grown up and your nest is empty. Children are supposed to grow up and leave home; it's always sad when a child, for whatever reason, isn't able to do that. For parents it is both a time of celebration and a time of sadness.

Each year as Ethan's birthday draws near, my memories of him come flooding back to me. We celebrate that day with his favorite birthday meal; beef and noodles and angel food cake. As I made numerous batches of homemade noodles today, I was listening to Pandora. The first song that played was "Brown-eyed Girl". It's become the "hello, Mom" song. I can't imagine how I would get through life, especially the hard days like his birthday, without knowing he is so near to me. I know so many other people don't have that comfort; I always wish I could help them find it.

I no longer live in the town where my husband and I raised our three sons. When suppertime comes now, I prepare it in a different kitchen and just for the two of us. There are many times when I'm preparing something I used to make during those years of cooking for my children, that I'm suddenly transported back to that kitchen; back to those days when one by one they would return home, as the sun began to set and the streetlights came on, up and down Olive St. When this sensation comes over me, I can actually feel myself in that kitchen. All of my senses are awakened to that moment in time. I can feel the water running over my hands, as I stand at the sink. I can feel the wooden spoon I'm stirring with. I can feel the table and hear the sound, as I place the plates on it. I can smell the aroma of whatever I'm cooking. These "memory trips" are always soothing to me. Those were good times; happy memories for me. My family was intact and I was happy and hopeful of a bright future and long life for each of us, and so it should have been. However comforting those "memory trips" are, I know I can't let myself linger there too long. Life must be lived in the present. I am blessed to feel Ethan's presence with me every day and I know one day my family will be together again.

WILL IT GO ROUND IN CIRCLES?

Have you ever seen the guy at the circus who spins the plates on sticks? Perhaps, this is one of those references that truly speaks to my age, but I hope someone who reads this will get the reference and I hope even more everyone will get the point.

I used to place great value on my ability to multi-task; to do as many things at once as I could manage. It made me feel so efficient and efficiency is something I have always valued.

The first problem with spinning plates is that it is an outward picture of what is occurring in your mind and spirit at the same time. While the outward appearance is efficiency, the inner reality is turmoil.

The next problem is that once you start spinning plates and discover you're pretty good at it; you want to keep adding another plate and then another. In order to successfully do this, it requires all of your mental focus and once you start, it's hard to stop, without having the plates crash to the floor and break into pieces. The scenario of calmness and order on the outside and turmoil inside is a reversal of living a spirit-filled life. There will always be a degree of turmoil in the outside world, but your spirit will only flourish in an environment of quiet, stillness and peace. Quiet and stillness are not exactly the same thing. Quiet means there is no noise on the outside that is distracting you. Stillness is a slowing down or calming of the senses within and then the spirit.

The space you create inside yourself to nurture your spirit, is yours to control. Even when the world outside you is at its most chaotic, you can remain calm and peaceful in your "sacred space". Doing this also requires your mental focus. Of course, there are times when the greater measure of mental focus must be turned to the problems of the outside world; such as solving a problem at work or caring for a sick child. There are many things that pull your focus back into the world, but knowing you can take a quiet, rebalancing break by returning to your "sacred inner space" helps to keep you calm on the outside, in times of stress or chaos.

There are times when I pray for more energy to accomplish the tasks before me, but I know I must be careful not to devote that extra energy to adding additional plates to spin. Keeping my schedule at a reasonable level was something I struggled with for many years. I was sacrificing inner peace for the sense of self-worth I felt from being skilled or crazy enough to keep the plates all spinning. It gave my confidence a big boost to be able to add one more plate (or task) to an already over-filled schedule. I felt guilty if I hadn't filled nearly every minute of every day with something, I believed was constructive. I needed something to show for the time that had passed that day. The more plates there are spinning, the faster they have to spin, so that you have time to move from one to the next to keep them from falling when they slow down. It's a lot like a dog chasing its tail; at the end of every day I just felt exhausted.

I'm not sure why we allow society (other people) to pressure us into living such chaotic lives. We all want to fit in so badly, to measure up to the expectations, others set; there is no peace to be found in that.

It was only when I found myself devastated by the tragedy of losing my son, that I let all of that go. I was physically, mentally, emotionally and spiritually unable to devote myself to living that way anymore. Everything slowed to a mere crawl as I focused on healing my heart and spirit. I was fighting for my own life and I had no energy or focus to give to anything else. During that time, I needed quiet and I needed to be still. Just because a space is quiet doesn't mean your spirit is calm and still. There are numerous ways to achieve stillness. Many people suggest meditation, which is something I've not been very successful with. I usually just turn everything off, close my eyes and breathe deeply. Almost instantly, I feel my heart rate begin to slow and the tension in my body begin to relax. I like listening to soothing music, reading poetry or my Bible, or just trying to bring my consciousness closer to the center of my body. After only a few minutes, I feel relaxed and refreshed and ready to get back to whatever I need to do. I have read many books about relaxation techniques etc. and many of them talk about creating a "sacred space or sanctuary" where you can step away from the busyness of the world to regain your spiritual balance.

If we use the ministry of Jesus as an example; He often retreated to a place of solitude to escape the ever-pressing demands and noise of the throngs that sought His wisdom and counsel. He secluded Himself when He wanted to pray and restore His spirit. We need to make time in our busy lives to do the same. Then, even when the world around us is going at dizzying speed and the noise quotient threatens to deafen us, we will find calm and stillness. My personal favorite times to pause and reflect, are early in the morning before the world is fully awakened and late at night when the harassed and weary inhabitants of the planet have fallen into exhausted sleep.

So, put the plates back in the cabinet and the sticks on the scrap pile and don't give up your new-found peace for anything!

TWILIGHT TIME

One of the things I've learn over the course of the past eight years (since my 60th birthday), is that we are all living our lives too fast. Younger people don't seem to realize that people haven't always lived life at break-neck speed. If you point that out to many of them, their first thought is, "Wow, that must have been really boring!" I guess you're not likely to miss what you've never had. I personally long for a slower, quieter life and something told me several years before my son's life was taken, to go back to that quieter place in life, as much as it is possible to do so. It isn't that you're liable to find that place somewhere if you go looking for it. It's something you have to consciously create for yourself. I have lived my life the past few years in very determined fashion to apply the brakes often.

My two most treasured times of day are dawn and dusk; twilight. At dawn the world is just beginning to awaken to a brand- new day. There is a quote from the Anne of Green Gables books where Aunt Marilla states: *"Tomorrow is always fresh, with no mistakes in it."* At dusk the world is slowing its pace for the end of the day. Both are such quiet, peaceful times. I have learned how to create quietness for myself, whether it be in my external surroundings or internally, no matter where I am or what is taking place.

I have to admit, I rarely get out of bed early enough to see the sun come up and where I now live there are lots of trees that obstruct the view if I do, so the only time I really have a good view of sunrise is in Autumn after the leaves have fallen or in early Spring before the trees have fully leafed out.

I do try to rise early enough to have at least an hour to devote to quiet pursuits such as praying, writing and reading. It really helps to set the tone for the rest of my day and reminds me that God is with me every day all day long.

I grew up in the 50's and 60's in a small midwestern town. It was a place where everyone knew their neighbors; people rarely locked their doors. As a child I enjoyed a degree of freedom that, sadly, my grandchildren will never know. We were often allowed to play outside during the summer months until long after dark, with no adults standing by to make sure we were safe. It was taken for granted that we were safe you could actually do that then. Sometimes we played at the city park until after 10pm, again, without supervision. The park was about 12 blocks from our home. It was as though the entire community took responsibility for its children. We could have gone to nearly any door to ask for help if we needed it. Strangers rarely came there and if they did, they drew enough attention that you always felt there were numerous pairs of eyes watching out for you. Sometimes, we weren't so happy about that, when Mrs. So and So, down the street, reported to your mother that she'd seen you walking with some boy!

Summer evenings hold a special place in my memory. Days were hot, dry and dusty and no one in our neighborhood had air conditioning in their home. The neighbors across the street had a large box cooler that was called a "Squirrel cage". The woman who lived there would let us come in and watch cartoons on particularly hot summer afternoons. Adults rose early to get their daily chores done and then rested in the heat of the day. After Supper, when the sun was setting and the breeze began to cool off, people would come out of their homes to enjoy the evening. It was about the same time the lightning bugs (fireflies) began to shine their tiny lights all over the neighborhood.

We lived half a block from my mother's aunt and uncle; Anna and Richie Wilbur. Richie was gifted with a talent for making many things. One of those things was a large wooden bench that sat in their yard, just in front of the flower garden and between their house and Mrs. Taylor, the next- door neighbor. I imagine there had been many benches in that spot over the years and that as soon as one wore out, another took its place. The bench was a gathering spot most evenings in summer and fall. Neighbors would often wander over to the bench to share some news, or a story and it seemed that one would leave and the next one would seize their opportunity to sit with Anna and Richie for a bit of conversation.

Many times, we as kids, would play games nearby; old fashioned games like, Crack the Whip, Ring Around the Roses or Tag; we would often just sit and listen to the stories that were being told. Eventually, our mother would call us home to bed and we were always reluctant for the evening to end. Whenever I sit outside in the evening and hear the crickets chirp, it reminds me of the long- ago days of my childhood on Pine St. The days were lived slowly and the evenings were savored, until suddenly that time passed away, as all things and all times must surely do.

THE BENCH

As Summer's sun begins to set;
My memories delight me yet;
Evenings spent in days gone by;
A million stars, within the sky.

Built of nails, paint and wood;
A staple of my neighborhood;
Where friends would come at close of day;
To laugh and talk the hours away.

Where happy children played nearby;
Where crickets chirped their lullaby;
A wooden bench, an evening breeze;
Where neighbors met to take their ease.

Their work was hard, they rose at dawn;
They gathered there upon the lawn;
They shared their joys and sorrows too;
They talked of things they'd yet to do.

They talked sometimes of death and life
They talked of happiness and strife;
They talked of loved ones, far and near;
They talked of those no longer here.

They talked of gardens, needing rain;
They talked of joy and sometimes pain;
They shared it all in such a way;
We sadly don't in this new day.

J.S. Schmidt -July 30, 2019

This poem is dedicated to Anna and Richie Wilbur and all of their neighbors on Pine Street.

I spoke earlier of my children's bonus grandmother; Anna was my own bonus grandmother. She was an incredibly unique spirit also. Though she had very little education, she had wisdom about so many things; she could heal animals who were sick or injured; she could walk outside and pick greens from her lawn to cook for Supper, that might have just looked like weeds to someone else; she knew which ones were safe to eat. She took care of sick and elderly people and she opened her home to several foster children; she made her own clothes on a treadle sewing machine, without the benefit of commercially made patterns; she could play the piano, though none of us remember there ever being one in her home. She could fold a piece of butcher paper, make a few snips with her scissors and when it was unfolded; she had a pretty decorative border for her kitchen shelves. She was a pretty good cook, though she never seemed to have any cookbooks around. She washed clothes in a galvanized metal tub on the back porch, scrubbed the stubborn spots on a washboard and hung everything on a clothesline. She cut and curled her own hair on curlers she made by cutting the cocoa can into strips with the tinsnips and then wrapping them in pieces of paper she cut from a brown paper grocery bag. She was an astute judge of character and a friend to nearly everyone who ever knew her.

This is my Great Aunt, Anna, holding me; she earned
the right to be called "Grandmother". My regret, is
that I never honored her that way in this life. I know
her spirit hears me say it now.

ADAM AT THE WINDOW

When I was still a young girl, around 8 or 9 years old; I would look down at the baby doll in my arms and think to myself: *"One day I'm going to hold a real baby of my own."* Time passed and since I had enough credits to graduate at the end of the first semester of my Senior year, I chose to do that. I married my high school boyfriend on my 17th birthday, just before school began that year. My oldest son was born 2 months before my 18th birthday; just prior to that pregnancy, I had a very early miscarriage. I hadn't even been aware that I was pregnant.

When I was a teenager, I thought that if I had a plan for my life, it must surely come true. Well, I did become a mother, but I had planned to only have female children. I had nothing against boys, but I grew up during the Vietnam War; when the draft was still in existence. I couldn't bear to think God would give me sons and they would be taken away to die in a war. Even at that young age, I realized every mother loves their child (at least they should) and that thousands of mothers had lost their sons in battle. Whenever I see an image of the Vietnam War Memorial, I think of all of those broken-hearted parents. Their grief touches me in such a personal way since my own child was taken from this life. My solution to this dilemma was that I would simply give birth to female children and not have to worry about such things. God planned otherwise!

As I mentioned earlier, my first pregnancy ended in a miscarriage, the second resulted in the birth of my son Brett, the third produced another son, Jeff and the fourth and last pregnancy, my son Ethan. After Brett and Jeff were born, I went through a divorce and had no intention of ever marrying again. I assumed there would be no more children and no possibility I would have a daughter, which had become incredibly important to me; I guess it was the psychological equivalent of "that which is denied, becoming the more desired thing."

When Tom and I married about ten months after my divorce, (so much for never marrying again), we decided to have a baby right away so our new baby wouldn't be separated from our other children in age, by too many years. Ethan was born 11 months after we married. During that pregnancy, I began to hope once more that I would have a daughter. I knew there was a good chance the child I was carrying would be another boy, but still I hoped and I put any other thought out of my head. I only considered girls names until shortly before the baby was due.

I succeeded pretty well with my delusion unless I ran into one particular person, a man I had known for many years, who liked to think he had a special insight into such things. Any time I saw him he would ask me: *"How is that little boy today?"* My reply was always:" *That's not a little boy!"* He would just smile and say: *"I know that's not what you want to hear, but it's the truth!"* One day I became really annoyed with him and I said: *"Oh, how would you know anyway?"* He just said, *"I know these things and besides, there are no little girls in you."* Now I was really insulted! Perhaps, he really does know what he's talking about?

Months later, my son Ethan was born after 4 trips to the hospital. The first 3 trips were false labor, which is just as painful as the real thing, but doesn't progress and gets you no closer to having a baby. By the time Ethan was actually born, I had convinced myself something had gone terribly wrong and he was going to be a stillbirth. When he was born and I heard him cry for the first time, I was so relieved to have a living, healthy child that it no longer mattered that he wasn't the girl I was hoping for. I had three healthy sons and decided not to press my luck any further. I had no more children. I stopped wandering through the little girl's section of every department store I went into. After Ethan was born, I began to think about what my friend had said: *"There are no little girls in you."* At some point, I realized that was true, but it took years for me to understand why it was true. Eventually, I realized that God knew I would be a better mother for boys and He gave me what I needed, instead of what I wanted. I accepted God's will and found peace with it.

Forty years later, when Ethan's life was taken and I was lost in deep grief, I had a vision of a little boy. It was just a quick flash, but the child spoke to me: "My name is Adam," he said. He was about 5-7 years old, with dark hair and eyes. My sons were all blondes, as children and had blue or green eyes. I began to wonder if Adam was the child I lost. The coloring didn't seem to fit, but one morning I woke and sat up in bed and I caught a glimpse of the pictures that hang on the wall next to my closet. They are the only pictures of myself that I like well enough to display. One is my Senior picture and the other my year-old portrait; I recognized that the baby girl in the picture had very dark hair and dark eyes, just like Adam. That isn't a name I would have considered, but he wasn't given a name in this world because it was such an early miscarriage. I like to think God gave him that name because he was the first of my male children, just as the biblical Adam is thought to be the first man. I know this will sound like a stretch to some people, but I have a deep sense of peace about it and that is the best measure of truth I know of.

CALLING MY CHILDREN HOME

Where have you gone;
My babies in blue?
I just closed my eyes;
How quickly you grew.

So small and precious in my arms;
Little faces, tiny hands and feet.
Nothing more I could have wanted;
These babies, that life, rich and sweet.

Smiling and laughing, together they grew;
Three little boys with dirt smudged faces;
Brothers, then and now and always;
Their love could fill the largest of spaces.

Where did they go? My three little ones;
I miss those happy, sweet little boys;
I miss the dirt, the fuss, the mess;
I even miss the fights and the noise.

But time has brought the saddest change;
Three you were, but now just two;
Hold the third lovingly in your heart;
Knowing he's there in whatever you do.

This isn't possible; real love doesn't die;
It's captured in your heart; it lives in your mind;
It lives forever in deep secret places;
That which seems lost; one day you will find,

I prayed God for children;
And He gave me you three;
How precious then; more precious now still;
The love and the joy God granted to me.

So broken and wounded;
My heart on that day;
But, God soothed and healed it
And grief's pain couldn't stay.

J.S. Schmidt- Dec.1, 2018

RAINY DAY PEOPLE

Have you ever known anyone who just seems to show up, out of the blue, at exactly the right moments? Someone who gives you strength, courage or peace just by being there for you? Perhaps, they say all of the right things at the right moment, or perhaps, they don't need to say anything at all? Perhaps, they are with you for all of the happy, joyous occasions in life? Perhaps, they haven't always been there for you, but in an unexpected, life-altering moment, you look up or look across a room and see them and know they have come to love and support you in your time of great need? I pray you have someone like this in your life!

Such a person as this is truly a gift from God; a gift of such magnificence, it's value cannot even be estimated. These are the kinds of gifts given to each of us by a loving and compassionate God. When I look back over the span of my years, I see many times that I benefitted from an appearance by the "Rainy Day People". You could just call them good friends, but no matter what you call them, they are a blessing.

I'd like to share some of my "rainy day" experiences with you...

The earliest one that comes to mind involves a very close friend I had in high school and for many years after, until our lives took very different paths and we drifted apart. I have previously mentioned my son Brett, who was born at the end of my Senior year. He was born with some hidden birth defects that were not immediately recognizable. After he came home from the hospital, he had problems digesting the formula the doctor recommended, so it was changed and then changed again two more times. The doctor was running out of suggestions and Brett was suffering from a condition known as "failure to thrive". My friend's mother who had seven children of her own, suggested I try to feed him goat's milk. Of course, I had visions of having to learn to milk a goat; I just knew I wouldn't be very good at that sort of thing, but she assured me you could buy goat's milk in a can right next to the evaporated milk, at the grocery store. As soon as I began giving him the goat's milk, he began to flourish and seemed like any other healthy baby. There were some other problems that crept up when he was about 16 months old, but no one, including the doctor put two and two together until he was much older. A few months before his third birthday, he got sick; really sick. After two weeks he was hospitalized with pneumonia and a major infection. It took another week to figure out where the infection was and what was causing it. Other doctors were called in to consult and they arrived at the conclusion that he had a non-functioning kidney (a birth defect) and it was the source of the infection. It needed to come out as soon as we could get him to a major medical center, in Kansas City.

The hospital was a huge scary place about two-hundred miles from our home and I was going to be there for at least a couple of weeks, by myself. My son Jeff was about six months old and I had to leave him with a sister-in-law; I had never been away from him overnight and he didn't take to many people other than myself and my sister, who was still in high school. It was one more thing weighing heavily on my mind.

A couple of days after the surgery, I came out of my son's room and looked down the long hallway as the elevator door was opening. There stood my friend Stacy and her 2yr, old son. They had come to be with me and were able to stay four days. Neither of us had any money for a hotel room and they had to sleep in the waiting room or on folding chairs in Brett's room, like I had been doing. We barely had money to eat, but I remember how happy I was to have them there with me at such a time of uncertainty. My son recovered and has been amazingly healthy to this day.

Many years later, we were told my mother's cancer was terminal and she had only weeks to live. My sister and I took care of her day and night at my parent's home, under the guidance of hospice nurses; it was emotionally depleting and physically exhausting. One afternoon, when we had been keeping vigil for about a month, the doorbell rang unexpectedly; when we opened the door there stood two of our oldest and dearest friends. Jeanne and I share several old friends; somehow, I think that's probably not a common thing. My sister and I weren't close until we were in our mid to late twenties and these friendships predate that time.

The two friends who came to visit that day are also sisters; Shirley is my age and Sandy is Jeanne's age. They are not people we see often and haven't for many years because we all live in different places now. They are the kind of friends that walk right in after years apart and the conversation seems to pick up right where it left off. They are two of the funniest people I know; they play off of each other like a great comedy team.

On the day they came to my mother's house, we were about three weeks away from the end of her life. Our emotions had been numbed by watching her life slipping away day by day and from the horror of seeing the damage cancer can do to a human being. If ever we needed a good laugh, it was on that day. I know that sounds disrespectful, given the circumstances and I felt that way too; at first.

We sat in Mother's living room and talked for several hours. Mom's hospital bed was set up in the corner and it had become her whole world. Sandy and Shirley began telling us about a recent vacation they had taken with their large extended family. They told a story about Shirley having to be coerced into going horseback riding with some of the other people present. Everyone tried to convince her it would be fine and she'd have a good time; even the horse's owner assured her that the horse they'd picked for her couldn't run if it wanted too. She reluctantly climbed on the old nag and was no more than seated when it took off at full gallop. It was the funniest story I've ever heard; mostly because they were telling it. We were laughing so hard we were crying. I felt so terrible to be laughing like that, when my mother was dying right before my eyes, so I suggested we leave for a while to get something to eat. Dad could stay with Mother and we would be back soon. I went over to the bed where Mother was laying and bent down to tell her we were leaving and would soon return. She motioned for me to come closer and then whispered in my ear *"I had the most wonderful afternoon!"* and she gave me a big smile. I was shocked! I thought we were being insensitive and upsetting her. My mother had a quirky sense of humor, so she loved the story about the runaway horse. She had a way of always trying to lighten everything up if things got too gloomy. Once when her mother was pre-planning her own funeral, my mother offered to lay down in a casket so Grandma could see what she would look like in it. They looked so similar they could have been sisters, I was horrified, but the two of them giggled about it for hours.

Laughter was what we needed most on the day Sandy and Shirley came to visit. I no longer believe in coincidence and I know God uses people to share joy and sorrow in this way. I know He brought Sandy and Shirley to Mother's front porch that day.

To everything there is a season;
And a time to every purpose under heaven;
A time to be born and a time to die;
A time to weep and a time to laugh;
A time to mourn and a time to dance.
Ecclesiastes 3:2 and 4

Sandy and Shirley paid us another timely visit, thirteen years later on what would have been Ethan's fortieth birthday; two weeks after his life was taken. It was another day to mingle grief with laughter. We sat on the porch of the big Victorian home Tom and I lived in, on a beautiful autumn afternoon. The porch ran the full length of the front of the house. It was about 10 ft' wide and there were several groupings of furniture that accommodated quite a number of people. On this particular day, we chose a pair of benches that faced each other; each pair of sisters occupied a bench together. We spent several hours there reminiscing about times we shared in the past.

Jeanne and I share another friend, Debra. We have been with her through the loss of both of her parents, a step-daughter and the general ups and downs of adult life. We have shared many times of sorrow, but many more times of fun and laughter. We were planning to have lunch together on the day I received the phone call that Ethan's life had been taken. She and Jeanne were the first people I called and they were there within minutes. She has been there for us as we buried our parents and my son. Friends that are always there to be your "Rainy Day People" are an indescribable blessing.

"THE RAINY DAY"

The day is cold, and dark and dreary;
It rains and the wind is never weary;
The vine still clings to the mouldering wall;
And the day is dark and dreary.

My life is cold, and dark and dreary;
It rains and the wind is never weary;
My thoughts still cling to the mouldering past;
But the hopes of youth fall thick in the blast;
And the days are dark and dreary.

Be still, sad heart! And cease repining;
Behind the clouds is the sun still shining;
Thy fate is the common fate of all;
Into each life some rain must fall;
Some days must be dark and dreary.

Henry Wadsworth Longfellow

PEACE

The love of God;
To my heart brings peace;
In Jesus arms;
I find release.

To my broken heart;
The Spirit speaks;
And fills me with;
The calm I seek.

I place my hand;
In the Savior's own;
I've never walked;
This world alone.

Through all my days;
Through all my years;
His boundless love;
Will dry my tears.

Until at last;
My soul shall rest;
Beyond the sun;
Among the blest.
J.S. Schmidt- May 30, 2019

100

THE CHURCH IN THE WILDWOOD

I chose this song as the title of this chapter, because it always makes me think about the church my father ministered at during my childhood and adolescent years. Every Sunday morning, we were rousted out of bed early, so we could make it on time, to the little country church we attended. It was nearly a forty- mile drive from our home. The church was located in the Flint Hills of Kansas, in a wide spot in the road that was known as, "Wonsevu". It is a Native American word that means, "running deer". Wonsevu was never really much of a town, though in some historical references, it's described as an "inland hamlet". When we attended church there, it consisted of about 4 buildings; the church and hall, an abandoned school building and what appeared to be the remains of a general store and gas station. There were also a few houses nearby.

People who attended the church, came from the farms and ranches that dotted the surrounding countryside. Though the official name of the church was Wonsevu Christian Church, it was really a community church, which I would define as a church of people of many faiths who come together because of proximity and generally overlook doctrinal differences. On a good day the attendance at the little church could run close to 40 people.

The song; "Church in the Wildwood" refers to a little brown church in the vale. A vale is a descriptive word for a valley. The church at Wonsevu did not sit in a valley; It was actually at an intersection and it was a very small, simple wooden structure that was painted white. It still had a steeple with a bell in it when we first started attending there. The church building consisted of a vestibule and one long open room. Classrooms were created by curtains hung on a wire and drawn on either side of a low stage, where the pulpit sat. There was no restroom and no running water. Baptisms took place in the creek down the road or in another church, in a nearby town. Even though I fussed pretty regularly about having to go (especially in a car with no air conditioner); years later I began to see it as an experience of simplicity and charm.

It was in that little country church that I developed my deep love of beautiful old church hymns. I have to confess I have little appreciation for today's "praise" music. Those old songs spoke to my heart in a way that sermons rarely did. I can't remember a single sermon I heard there, but I still remember a lot of the words to those old hymns.

The church had an old upright piano, that was almost always played by the same woman. Her name was Margaret and I can't even guess how many years she played for services there. She was a typical farm wife and the mother of 4 sons. One of the boys was born missing part of his forearm and hand. Margaret taught him to play the piano and occasionally they would play a duet together for church. I always thought that said so much about her as a mother and a human being; she taught her son that if he focused on what he could do and not on his limitations it would help him get through life. As soon as you got to know him, his disability became invisible. She was known as a "good Christian woman", which used to be considered about the highest compliment there was.

Those were much simpler times and church attendance held a place of great importance in the majority of homes. I often think people were happier back then, even though they worked harder and had fewer luxuries.

One of the highlights of attending Wonsevu Christian Church was the dinner that took place once a month after services. Those farm women were fabulous cooks and they went all out; fried chicken, homemade pies and cakes etc. It was heavenly!

Each Christmas, we kids were obliged to take part in the Nativity play on Christmas Eve. If you were one of the few girls, you knew you were either going to be an angel or Mary. Margaret and a woman named Doris provided enough boys to fill all of the roles of shepherds, wisemen and Joseph; we contributed our only brother to round out the cast.

Following the play there would be singing of Christmas carols and the reading of the Nativity story from the book of Luke, (always from the King James translation) and then a closing prayer. Since this always took place at night that meant another eighty- mile round trip to the church. Our much -anticipated reward at the end of the evening, was a small brown paper bag filled with old-fashioned candy, the kind that used to be made in small Mom and Pop shops. There was usually an orange or an apple to help fill the bag. We were always happy to share the candy with our father, who had an insatiable sweet-tooth.

The congregants of that little church were an eclectic mix of Quakers, Methodists, Baptists and even a Jehovah's Witness. Trying to bring a group of people of such varied doctrinal backgrounds together today could be disastrous, but in that little country church there was seldom any squabbling. These were people who wanted a sense of community; they were neighbors and friends. They needed each other and they knew it. They were the kind of people who helped each other in times of need. If a farmer was sick and couldn't work, they would come together to build the barn he couldn't finish or cut and bale his hay or cut his wheat and haul it to the elevator in town, using their own trucks and gas. They expected no payment other than a grateful handshake and the assurance of knowing that farmer would gladly do the same for them, if the situation was reversed. These were good, salt of the earth people, who came together in friendship and faith to worship at their little community church. They were some of the best people I've ever known.

My sister and I visited Wonsevu about a year ago; I wanted to see it again. It was in a sad state of disrepair. The church hasn't been used for many years. Nearly everyone who attended there is gone now. It is a place I hold only fond memories of. I have had to learn to accept many changes in life over the past few years, but I thank God for such precious memories as these.

BROTHER LOVE'S TRAVELING SALVATION SHOW

This song by Neil Diamond always reminds me of my grandfather, Roy Pierce. He was an ordained Baptist minister, among many other things. As a child, I attended a revival meeting where my grandfather preached. I remember sitting next to my grandmother as the congregation sang, "When the Roll is Called Up Yonder"; it was the only time I remember hearing her sing. I have read that Neil Diamond wrote this song thinking he was dismissing the idea of revival meetings actually touching people in a spiritual way, only to discover there was actually something powerful there.

Grandad was also a carpenter, who built pumice stone houses; often for people who really couldn't pay him much. He would accept nearly any form of payment and once I believe, someone paid him for work he had done for them, with a milk cow. Because he often worked as a carpenter, his hands were always rough and he had a blood blister somewhere, every time we saw him. He built the home I grew up in and knowing he had built it, made it even more special to us. He was a farmer from time to time, a railroad worker, a county employee and for a time a restaurant owner.

He was born in Marion County, Virginia in 1898. His mother's father was an ordained minister who was well educated for the time and served several different denominations over the course of his ministry. My grandfather was the oldest of ten children. There were some in the family who suspected he was his mother's favorite child. I don't know if that was a fact she admitted to or if it was something those close to her just believed to be the case. I have often heard that any mother's favorite child is the one who needs them most in any given moment; far be it from me to argue that point.

Grandad's mother, Lucy Lee (Kirk) Pierce was a zealously religious woman and when her eldest child entered the ministry, she was quite proud of his decision.

Roy married at the age of 18 and he and my grandmother, Flora Dell (McKinley) Pierce, soon began raising their own large family. They were blessed with 8 children. My own father was one of a set of twins born to them, after the births of 4 daughters. They had almost given up the idea that they would have a son and then God gave them two at once.

Following his ordination, my grandfather continued to work at his various occupations during the week, but his dedication to the ministry occupied much of his thinking. He had little education and his handwriting wasn't the best, so my grandmother would write out his sermons for him. How he found time to compose them and how she, the mother of eight children, found time to write them, has always been a mystery to me.

On Sunday mornings Flora would rise very early and prepare breakfast. Breakfast for Grandad almost always included homemade biscuits. He claimed he could judge the character of a man by whether he knew the right way to eat a biscuit. After breakfast, Flora had the task of getting the children ready to head off to church. The older girls would help, but it was still hard to get everyone, including herself, out the door on time. When everyone else was ready to go, she could finally spend a few minutes making herself presentable. For most of her life she had very long hair that she wore in two long braids, which were wrapped around the back of her head and pinned in place. She usually had one "good" dress that was suitable for church or funerals, so at least there wasn't the problem of wondering what she should wear. Imagine how much time that would save all of us. As Roy, who was only responsible for getting himself to church on time, rushed out the door, he would always shout over his shoulder, *"Come on, Mother, we'll be late!"*

One of the churches he served late in his ministry, was in the little town of Dexter, Ks. It was a fair distance from their home and many times they would make the trip on Saturday afternoon and spend the night in the parsonage the church provided. In those days there was no air conditioning in the church, so on Sunday morning all of the church windows were opened as wide as possible to let whatever breeze there might be flow through. Grandad had a very loud, booming voice and he wasn't a person who would ever have needed a microphone.

There was a house next door to the church; right next door! The windows of the house would all be open as well. One day the owner of that house had gone to town to run some errands and one of the local business owners asked him if he had ever heard Reverend Pierce preach? His reply was;" *Well, we don't need to go to church for that, we can hear every word he says sitting in our own home."*

Grandad also loved to sing with that loud, booming voice. He owned two accordions, that were probably his most treasured possessions. They looked tiny in his large hands and when he played them, he held them in the air away from his body and gave them a real workout! When my father's family would get together there was always music and laughter. There was an old piano in the corner of Grannie's living room and sometimes my mother would play cords on it while my Dad and his brother would play guitars and Grandad would play his accordion. Once, someone asked Grandad if he could play piano, since it had a similar keyboard to the accordion, his reply was, *"Only if you turn it on its side!"*

Grandad did nearly everything with gusto! He occasionally would visit the church where my father served as pastor and play his accordion and sing. I have a very vivid memory of him singing the old hymn:" Power in the Blood" and as usual, he gave it his all! The accordions were given to my father after Grandad passed away, probably because he was the one who could play them. They in turn were passed down to me and my sister, even though neither of us could play them. I am so proud to own the one I received; it was the one I most often heard him play. I wish I could hear that very distinctive sound just once more, because I associate it so closely with my grandfather. The accordion I have is damaged from so much use over the years and leaks air, so it makes no sound; I love it nevertheless.

In 1955, Roy and Flora suffered the death of their oldest child, Lucy. She was 38 yrs. old. That loss tested Rev. Pierce's faith as nothing ever had before and for a time he turned away from God. My father told me when I was very young that God understands grief and He will wait for us to turn back to Him, no matter how long it takes. Grandad was able to work through his grief and his faith sustained him through many years, until he himself passed on.

Roy left this life just a couple of days after he and Flora celebrated 50 yrs. of marriage. On Sunday, before his passing, he had seen nearly every member of his large extended family, at the party held in their honor. Soon after Roy's passing, Grannie began to tell us that he had been coming to visit her and at one point she had seen him just outside the door, on the patio. Nearly everyone dismissed her claims as wishful thinking; Grannie wasn't one for imagining things. She was about as down to earth as a person could be, so I chose to believe her.

When Ethan's life was taken, I knew I had been right to believe the things Grannie said she saw and heard. On the morning of Ethan's service, as I stood looking into the mirror in the upstairs bathroom, I suddenly felt Grandad's presence behind me. I felt him wrap his arms around me in a gesture of total love and support. I know he was telling me he understood my pain, because he too had lost a precious child. I didn't see him; I only felt and sensed his presence. I know without question he came to comfort me.

As soon as I began speaking publicly about my experiences, following the loss of my son, other people began to share similar stories with me. So many say they are afraid to talk about these spiritual encounters and it is a relief to be able to share them with someone who doesn't question their validity.

My Dad would tell Grannie she was only seeing what she wanted to see. In a sense, he was right, because I don't believe these things happen to those who aren't receptive to them. That does not mean she imagined it and it didn't really happen. I believe it's possible, in the right circumstances, for these things to happen to everyone.

I miss Grandad's booming voice, his Santa Claus laugh, and his huge rough carpenter's hands. I look forward to seeing him again someday!

WALK ON

Walk on, sweet child;
Walk on without fear.
It may be the next step;
That finds you in the clear.
The course of a life;
One step, and then another;
Will soon be revealed;
Said dear old Grandmother.
Days of sunshine or sorrow;
The path must surely be trod;
Perhaps today; perhaps tomorrow;
Beneath the gaze of God.
First one step and then another;
Some steps easy; many steps hard;
Some with sister; some with brother;
One step leading to the next.
Some steps in pain; some steps in joy;
Some steps in grief; some steps in fear;
Some steps together; both a girl and a boy;
But onward; ever onward;
This path of life you tread;
Till you stand in the clearing;
With the sunlight overhead.
Till all is sweet serenity;
Not a cloud up in the sky;
Not a tear; nor a sorrow;
Not an if only; or a why?
Step by step; it all lies behind you;
The life you were blessed to live;
Step on now; to another brand new;
You completed the journey;

The circle of life.
Walk on; where others walked before;
Through dark and dismal valleys;
Who slipped silently through heaven's open door;
Where pain and darkness; turn to light.
Where all is joy and peace and love;
And all is restored as once it was;
A Holy place...
J.S. Schmidt-Jan. 2, 2019

FLORA'S SECRET

I wrote the poem, "Walk On" in memory of my paternal grandmother, Flora Dell McKinley- Pierce. We always called her "Grannie", in fact, nearly everyone called her Grannie. I was ten years old when I asked my father if she had a real name.

Flora was born in Jamestown, Kentucky, on April 21, 1900. Her mother passed away when she was 5 yrs. old, she was the oldest of four siblings, and in very short order, she had a step-mother who began to have a number of children. Her step-mother seemed cold when compared to the mother she lost, but I guess you could counter that thought by realizing her step-mother, Cora, was probably overwhelmed in the beginning, to be taking on four very young children and before she adjusted to that her own children began to be born, in pretty rapid succession. As the oldest, Flora helped care for all of the younger children, yet she often felt alone and longed to have her own children.

She met her future husband, (my grandfather) at church after her family had moved to Oklahoma from Kentucky. Her father disapproved of the attention she was getting and tried to keep her and her young suitor apart. They eloped in a horse and buggy with the help of sympathetic friends. Roy was 18 and Flora was 16 yrs. old. They were married 50 yrs. and had 8 children. Flora lived to be 96 yrs. old. During her life she saw many changes in technology and science. She lived through two World Wars, the sinking of the Titanic, the Great Depression, the Dust Bowl and the moon landing. She had a great interest in life and learning, though her education came to an abrupt halt when she married young and had a family; she didn't stop trying to educate herself by reading and watching television, until the last few years of her life. She also lived through floods, fires, poverty, failed crops, failed businesses and the tough assignment of being the preacher's wife. She lost her oldest daughter in 1955 when she and her husband drowned in a nearby lake; It was a tremendous blow.

Watching Grannie cook and serve a meal was almost like watching a magic show. My family would sometimes go to Grannie and Grandad's house for lunch and a visit on Sunday, after church. My Dad had seven siblings and along with spouses and children, they would also be at Grannie's house for Sunday dinner; her house would be filled to overflowing. Sometimes people would bring a dish, but I remember her busying herself pulling little bowls of leftovers out of her fridge to add to whatever dishes she was preparing for the meal. Nearly everything she cooked came from the garden Grandad tended. We were always excited to learn she had made a boysenberry cobbler. The berries came from a thorny bush that grew at the corner of her house.

When at last the meal was served, everyone grabbed a plate and filled it. No two plates were alike, but there were always enough of them. We never worried about a place at the table; we just sat on the floor with our plate on our lap and ate her delicious food. No one could replicate what she cooked and get the same result. Everything she cooked had a distinctive flavor and I never figured out what she did to get it to taste that way.

When the meal was over and everyone was full, she would begin putting leftovers in those tiny little bowls and put them in the refrigerator. It always reminded me of the story of Jesus feeding the five thousand, with a few fish and a couple of loaves of bread. She had started with what looked like so little and fed so many, yet she always had leftovers to put away. To a young child it seemed miraculous. I think Grannie had many secrets!

Though she had little formal education, she was blessed with the kind of wisdom that doesn't come from books; it comes with living a hard life. She didn't say a lot, but gave good sound advice when asked. I was probably a young teenager when she told me this, *"No matter what trouble presented itself in my life, I just kept putting one foot in front of the other and pretty soon I had walked my way out of it."* That simple advice has served me well over the course of my own life. It has come to mind, at some point, in every time of trial I've experienced. I heard it in my mind over and over again after losing Ethan, as I tried to regain my balance. There were many days I didn't think I could live with the reality of that loss another minute and I would remember Grannie's words and put them into practice. She lived a simple life, worked hard, and trusted God to take care of her, here and in the hereafter. She was ordinary and incredibly unique.

BIRD ON THE MOUNTAIN

Once I walked to the top of a majestic mountain;
In solitary thought I trod; in belief I was alone.
Coolest water thirst did quench; a gift from a natural
fountain.
Drinking my fill; I stopped to rest and sat upon a stone.

Above the clouds; the sun shone bright;
Softest breezes, gently touched my face.
I heard God's whisper in the warmth and light.
Had I in sadness, stumbled on a secret Holy place?

A question then; a voice so rich, as none I'd ever heard;
Simply put, to me He asked:
"Tell Me why you're here?"
The voice had come, it seemed, from a splendid, regal
bird;
Soaring freely above my head; across the sky so clear.

*"Came I here, with thoughts confused; to try to find the
stillness.*
Came I here, in fear of death and grief to find my peace.
*Came I here, in sickness racked; to escape the grip of
illness.*
*Came I here, with troubled heart and spirit; to find the gift
of grace.*

"Indeed, I see," now said the bird, as He flew so high
above.
*"And now, pray tell me, if you please, whatever did you
find?"*
"All I sought and even more, of beauty, peace and love."

To the marvelous bird I answered back, in cheerfulness sublime.

"And is that all?" He then inquired, with beady eye askance.
"Oh no! Not all, I then replied; Not all, but just the least!"
"The best I found, my sovereign God; really quite by chance;
And so, at last, all fear is gone and faith is now increased."

He pondered then a moment, His head all cocked askew;
"I thought so!" then He whispered, from deep inside a cloud.
Many who come to this mountain, find that life is made anew,
So, no more let fear find you, when storms of life clash loud."
"I soar above you always, on wings stretched out in flight;
So, live your life in peace and never live with fear;
You'll never be abandoned; nor ever out of sight;
I am in you and around you; always and ever near."

J.S. Schmidt- Mar. 4, 2018

116

LEAVING ON A JET PLANE

My spirit has no doubt as to where the living spirit of my departed son is now residing; my heart on the other hand sometimes gives in to wishful thinking. Even after 4yrs. the events that led to Ethan's passing often seem so surreal; it feels like I've been living a bad dream since that day. My heart longs to deny the truth and tells me occasionally, that perhaps, Ethan is just living somewhere else on this planet and I should try to find him. I'm sure that doesn't sound quite rational, but bear in mind that my brain doesn't buy into that thought, any more than my spirit does. My heart just struggles to believe the awful truth.

I have so many memories of Ethan waiting for me to get off a plane, at the Lubbock airport or the Memphis airport and my heart wants to believe if I could just find the right airport somewhere in the world, he would be standing outside the gate waiting for my arrival; just as in days past.

Ethan was the reason I developed the courage to get on an airplane to begin with; I had an inexplicable fear of flying, all of my life. I thought I would be claustrophobic and clawing to get out, or the experience would be so terrifying that once the plane landed, I would refuse to get back on it; even if that meant I had to walk home from another state.

I knew as soon as Ethan accepted a teaching position at Texas Tech, that I would have to get on a plane, if I wanted to see him or his family, more than twice a year. It was nearly a ten- hour drive from our home in Kansas and I was used to seeing them about every six weeks. Much to my surprise, I discovered I didn't really mind flying. I've never had a really bad experience in the air and if I had, I'm sure I might feel differently.

I have many memories of walking through the doors into the terminal and seeing Ethan's face light up, when he saw me. My heart longs for that experience; to be able to see his face, alive and animated; to look into his eyes, to touch him and see the smile on his face.

I know, as a mother, I have been infinitely blessed in being able to hear Ethan speak to me, from the place he is now residing and to feel his presence in a room with me. I wish every mother longing for her lost child could have those experiences. All I have the power to give to others is the knowledge that these things are possible; I hope that is some comfort to those who need it.

In the early days of my grief, it comforted me to think Ethan had just gone on a trip to a destination we would all arrive at, over a period of time. I associated that thought with the John Denver song "Leaving on a Jet Plane" so, whenever I hear the song, it reminds me that Ethan has only gone to another place and we will see him, when we go there too.

I knew very early on in Ethan's life that his world would be infinitely larger than mine. I worked really hard to keep my world small. Ethan enthusiastically embraced every new place and experience. If they didn't come his way on their own, he would often orchestrate the encounter himself. I lived my life in fear of a number of things. Ethan never let fear or uncertainty chart his course. He was such an optimist and I was anything but that. He was always happy when he could drag me out of my "comfort" zone and show me my fears were unfounded. He could so easily pull you into his expansive enjoyment of life and all it has to offer those who live it fearlessly.

SILVER WINGS- THE AIRPORT

In my mind's eye, I see you;
Just there, outside the gate;
As I walk across the terminal;
Where patiently, you wait.

How often I have seen you;
With that smile that lit your face;
As I rush through sliding doors.
To share your warm embrace.

Are you waiting now?
In some far and distant place;
Or is it just my lonely heart;
Trying desperately to erase;

The distance now between us;
The pain, the grief, the tears?
I've lived and borne this longing;
Through months and then through years.

I know that you are happy.
I know that you're content.
I know this through the music;
Through the messages you've sent.

Truly, I know, that you exist;
In a place where the brilliant sun;
Is anxiously waiting in the East;
Till the dark of night, is finally done.

I know that you are waiting there;
Where raindrops full, stand by;
To nourish and restore the earth;
As heavy they fall, from a stormy sky.

I think, perhaps, I'll find you;
In God's rainbow, way up high;
As with such grace it arches;
Across the great blue sky.

My heart thinks I could find you;
Waiting at an airport, somewhere;
Though my mind knows that's silly;
My heart just doesn't care.

Someday, I know I'll find you;
In the place, where you wait;
I'll walk through the unknown valley;
And pass through the open gate.

As you wait there for my coming;
Another waits there too;
With love and great compassion;
He'll bring me then to you.

It's a face I still remember;
From the day upon the hill;
In the place we sadly left you;
So calm, serene and still.

Don't worry then He told me;
I hold him in My arms;
No one can ever hurt him;
He'll come to no more harm.

I'll hold him and I'll love him;
Until you reach the day;
When I'll walk you into heaven;
Forever more to stay.

J.S. Schmidt- Feb. 14, 2019
Valentine's Day

Professor Schmidt speaking to some students at Bennett Elementary School in Wolfforth, Texas, where Liz taught Kindergarten and Connor and Dylan attended.

ALL MY LOVIN'

When Ethan left this world, he was in the midst of raising his children. It was a role he cherished and it consumed so much of his heart, mind and soul. He was a very "hands on" father, from the moment his oldest son was born. He adored his two little boys and he was absolutely thrilled when he and Liz were told, their third child would be a girl. He wanted so much to experience fatherhood from every angle possible.

He would frequently call me late in the afternoon and I would ask him what he was doing. His reply was often," *I'm holding a sweet little girl, while she takes her nap.*" I would ask him, *"Will she wake up if you lay her down?"* and he would say," *Maybe, but I just love to hold her and watch her sleep."*

Ethan and Liz both loved reading to their children and would take turns with each child at bedtime, or sometimes they would just talk about whatever the kids had on their minds. When Ethan was taken from his family, everything became hard, but I think bedtime was particularly hard for the kids. My grandchildren have been such a comfort to me and I have tried my best to be a comfort to them; I am so blessed to have them. Often, in talking with other parents who have lost a child, they will tell me how much they wish they could have grandchildren from the child they love and miss. I feel their pain and I understand how that would feel. I know they would willingly endure the pain I have felt, when my granddaughter cried and wanted her Daddy and it made me feel so helpless and inadequate. I often sit in an auditorium or a gymnasium and wish my grandchild could look out into the audience, or up in the bleachers and see their Dad, beaming with pride. It makes one feel so powerless to know you could probably give them anything; except the one thing they so desperately want.

Ethan's daughter was five years old, when his life abruptly ended. Like so many little girls, she absolutely adored her Daddy. I remember how safe I always felt when my Daddy was nearby; losing him at age 90, was still so painful. I miss him so much and I can't imagine having to grow up without him in my life.

On the day we had to leave Ethan at the cemetery and return home without him, reality began to set in for all of us. Later that day, my son, Jeff, wanted to return to the cemetery to change out the marker with Ethan's name on it. Because we had to deal with two mortuaries, each one had prepared a temporary marker and Jeff thought the one we had at home was nicer. It had a picture of Ethan and a short paragraph about who he was, a devoted family man and a friend to nearly everyone he ever met. When Jeff announced his decision to go back to the cemetery, nearly everyone wanted to go with him. My husband and I stayed at the house because we were exhausted and there were still people there. It was many months, before Tom would willingly go with me to the cemetery; It is still a very hard thing for him, emotionally.

It was nearly 7pm, when they arrived at the cemetery and found the gate was locked; they parked the car and climbed over the fence. They walked up to where Ethan was and as they stood there together, someone looked up and saw a pink heart-shaped balloon flying toward them. It was losing altitude and the kids began to chase it to try and catch it. It came down within the bounds of the cemetery and Ethan's son, Connor, reached up and grabbed the string that was tied to it. He gave it to Brianna; it was a "princess" balloon. Brianna was one of those little girls who loved all of the princesses. She had princess dresses, princess dolls, princess sheets, princess nightgowns etc. She believed Daddy sent her that princess balloon. She loves to do balloon launches to Daddy and often we write notes to attach to them.

Now, some would say, "Oh, you just try to make something out of everything". Picture this scene: A little girl, who's just lost the father she adores, happens to be standing beside his grave, at the very moment a pink child's balloon happens to come floating down out of the sky to her. You can think what you will. I no longer believe in coincidence; I've seen too many things. It wasn't a red balloon that said, "Happy Birthday, Grandpa or a green balloon that said, Happy Bar Mitzvah. It was a pink princess balloon, that pretty much fell right into a little girl's hands, at a very special moment in time.

You could talk for years and never convince me, that didn't happen by design.

PRINCESS BRIANNA

Precious little princess;
No matter where you are;
Remember, Daddy loves you;
He's never really far.

As he sends it to you now;
I hope you feel his love;
As it gently floats to earth;
From the heavens up above.

He never meant to leave you;
That choice was not his own;
He wanted just to hold you;
To see you safely grown.

He sees you now from heaven;
He watches as you grow;
He sends you Daddy's kisses;
When you don't even know.

This is not the ending;
Though time is spent apart;
Remember, Daddy loves you;
And keep him in your heart.

J.S. Schmidt- May 21, 2019

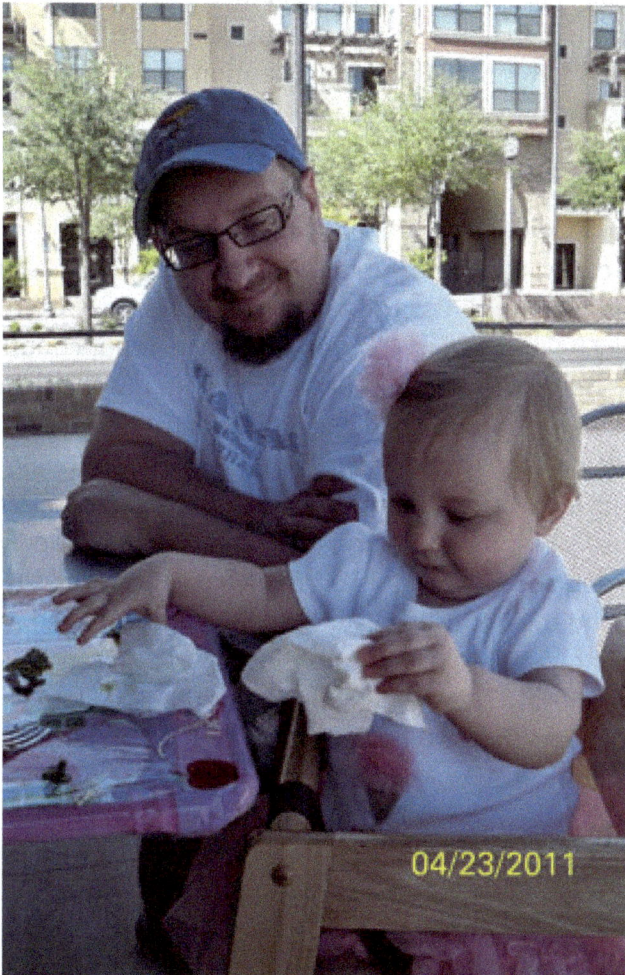

Daddy and Princess Brianna on her 1st
birthday.

INDEPENDENCE DAY

Today is July 4, 2020; Independence Day. The title of this chapter is a song that relays a fictitious event that occurs on July 4th; it is really to draw attention to domestic abuse. That is a very real and pervasive issue, but that's not what this chapter is about.

Every year at this time, as I observe a very large portion of people in this country, blowing up hundreds, and in many cases, thousands of dollars-worth of fireworks and partying their brains out, I ask myself how much attention is really being given to the remembrance of our country's independence from Great Britain? How many people are even aware that the holiday isn't just another opportunity to throw a big party for their family and friends, but was instead, intended to mark the incredible accomplishment of those who fought a war, where they were decidedly the underdog and which could certainly have just as easily produced the opposite result. Much blood was shed and many sacrifices were made so that we, today, can commemorate this day in History. For those of you who love the Fourth and who will certainly stand up and defend your right to celebrate and commemorate as you see fit, I will admit, it's not my favorite day of the year. I like it less, which means I try to tolerate it, at best, every year I live through it. I do have a lot of memories of past events that happened around the Fourth.

Our little hometown, celebrates Independence Day every year, with a fabulous, public fireworks show and has done so for over ninety years. The show is produced solely through the labor and expertise of local volunteers. At one time or another nearly everyone who ever lived there has participated in some fashion. On July 4th, our little town of about 1,400 would swell to somewhere in the neighborhood of 10-15 thousand for the duration of the fireworks display.

I grew up with the fireworks show as did my children and my grandchildren. When we were young, my siblings and I would anxiously wait to turn the page on the calendar, from June to July. About July 2, a caravan of tractor trailers and mobile homes would roll into town, that signaled the carnival for the celebration had arrived. The "carnies" would immediately set to work assembling all of the various rides and games of chance, ticket booths and other attractions; within hours our city park was transformed into an amusement park. It almost felt like a mirage, because as quickly as it came, it disappeared. That created a great sense of urgency on the part of the kids in town to get there as soon as they opened and ride as often as we talk our parents into the ticket money, until the last ride was shut down an hour or so after the last aerial had exploded and lit up the sky over the football stadium.

Even as a child, I was never that excited about the fireworks you could buy to shoot off on your own. My brother was pretty crazy about them, but he became a little less enthusiastic when a small firecracker called a "ladyfinger", exploded in his hand. He suffered no permanent damage, but he was much more careful after that. I was instantly cured of handling anything that could possibly explode.

My first memory of attending the fireworks show is when I was about 4-5 years old. My mother's Uncle Richie took us to the park before it was dark and parked his car across the road from the football field. He backed it in so we could sit on the fenders of his big green Dodge and watch the action. As soon as it was dark enough, the sky was filled with beautiful sparkling lights of every color. I didn't like the bombs that just made really loud noises and weren't pretty and I didn't like the sulfur smell of the thick smoke that filled the air.

A few years later, when our parents thought we were old enough to go by ourselves, my brother and I at last got to experience the carnival rides on our own. We each had our favorite; mine was the Tilt-A-whirl, my brother's, was the roller coaster. I was afraid of the roller coaster, but as usual, my brother talked me into going and he would make me laugh, so it wasn't as scary.

One year, we sat on the baseball field to watch the fireworks and thought we had a great spot, but the fireworks were damp from the rain the previous day and the humidity the rain created, so they didn't go off as planned. Some of them didn't go off at all and some that did, didn't climb to the height they were supposed to, before they exploded. There was almost no wind that night and the heavy air caused them to shower the crowd of spectators with hot embers. I still have a scar on my knee from the ash that landed on me that night.

Years later, I was a young teenager with a premature interest in boys; I went to the fireworks with strict orders from my mother that I was to stay with my girlfriends, and not go off anywhere with boys. I admit I had other things in mind. I was always interested in older boys; the ones I grew up with just didn't hold any fascination for me at all. A few weeks into the summer that year, a guy named Doug, came to visit his cousin for a couple of months. It wasn't really often that someone new came to town, so he was an instant hit with the girls. Foolishly, I decided to try to get his attention. I wasn't allowed to actually date, but my friend Linda and I managed to meet up with him several times anyway. It was a very short relationship; actually, about two weeks, but it served to teach me a number of valuable lessons. On the night of the Fourth, he was supposed to meet me at the carnival, in front of the Ferris Wheel at 9pm; I waited until about 10, before I admitted to myself, he wasn't coming. It was the one and only time in my life, I was stood up. Actually, I was ditched for somebody else, to be quite honest. The next morning, I heard that Doug and the girl he threw me over for, had been in a serious car accident with some of my other friends. The driver suffered a broken neck, but everyone else walked away with cuts and bruises. The accident could have taken their lives and I realized I could have been there too.

As I look back on that night, I realize also that it was another time that I was kept from harm, by something. You could call that something a guardian angel, or God, but you can't call it coincidence. I no longer believe in coincidence. I think nearly everyone reaches a time when they crave independence, whether they are mature enough to handle it or not. We consider it a rite of passage to grow up and leave the care of our parents and be free to make our own decisions and set our own course. Many of us, especially as adolescents, believe reliance on God's wisdom, interferes with our ability to live independent lives. I regret the length of time it took me to realize I had no wisdom or strength of my own, and ask for God's help. It was when I believed my life was destroyed on the day my son, Ethan was taken from me, that I admitted my inability to go it alone. Help came so swiftly and I am still amazed and humbled that all I needed to do was ask and then listen for and follow the guidance I was given.

CHISELED IN STONE

In the past few months as we've all tried to adjust to life in the midst of a pandemic, it has been hard not to see our family members face to face. All of the technology that allows us to see each other on facetime, zoom or skype, helps to make the situation more tolerable, but it is a poor substitute for actually sharing the same space with those you love.

My husband and I recently met my brother and his wife and one of my sisters, at a park in a small town that was about equal distance for all of us to travel. It happened to be a place where some of my mother's family lived for a number of years and some of them are buried in the cemetery there. We sat in our lawn chairs, socially distancing from each other, had the lunch we each brought and spent about four hours together. Before we left town, we visited the cemetery where our relatives are buried. We were sad to discover that one of our grandmother's brothers has no stone; there is nothing there that conveys the fact that he or anyone else is buried in that spot.

There are several reasons that I find that objectionable; the first goes back to a book I first read as a child, about Tutankamen, the boy Pharaoh of Egypt, who's tomb was discovered in the Valley of the Kings in 1922. I was instantly consumed with fascination for the Pharaohs and Egyptian history. I read that book over and over and to this day, I enjoy watching programs about the newest discoveries of Egyptian antiquities and the latest information that can be discovered with new scientific technologies, about even the oldest artifacts.

The ancient Egyptians believed it was vitally important that your name be immortalized in some way after you passed from life, and if it wasn't it was as though you had never existed. That held important consequences in their view of the afterlife. Many significant monuments in Egypt were severely damaged through the vindictive vandalism perpetrated by the successors to the throne of the Pharaoh. Often, they sought to totally eradicate the preceding ruler's existence by destroying any evidence in tombs, on buildings, statuary and writings that the former king had ever walked on the earth. It has taken centuries in many cases to unearth the history and factual order of the Egyptian dynasties. Destroying history, or even allowing it to be unrecorded, does a great disservice to humanity.

This is why, I believe every person who ever lived should have their name immortalized in some way. The most logical way to do that is on a grave stone. A name chiseled in granite is a long- lasting memorial to a life lived.

My sister, Jeanne and I have spent a lot of time wandering through cemeteries, wondering about the lives of those who rest beneath the often- beautiful remembrances, carved in stone. We would sometimes make tracings of the sentimental poems and quotes we found on them. We actually discovered a relative buried in our hometown cemetery, we didn't know about. As with anything you study closely, you can begin to see many things that don't appear obvious with just a cursory glance.

Many times, the tenderest words and most beautiful art appears on the stones of children, wives or mothers. Some cemetery art depicts symbols, the significance of which is known only to the loved ones who requested they be included. There are many different emotions reflected in the messages on grave stones. Our paternal great-grandmother's stone reads: *She hath done what she* could". We were always puzzled by what was meant by that; only quite recently we discovered through some genealogical research my sister was doing, that the same quote appears on the grave stone of our 3 times great-grandmother and it is scripture taken from Mark 14:8 which reads:" *She hath done what she could; she is come aforehand to anoint my body to the burying.*" It is a reference to the woman who anointed Jesus with expensive perfume, prior to his Crucifixion.

In our hometown cemetery, the stone of a Mr. W.D. Butler, who owned a hardware store, reads:" *An honest man is the noblest work of God*"- *Pope;* that is followed by this" *those who owed W.D. Butler at the time of his death, seriously ask themselves this question; Am I an honest man?*" This rather stingy-sounding, vindictive man, was also the person who left a large sum of money for the town's school children to be given a picnic every year at the end of school, at his expense. The quotes seem to convey the worst of his nature, while a little bit of research shows him to be as generous in some instances, as he seems tight-fisted and unforgiving in others. It is a good reflection of the complexity of human beings and the dangers of judging people based on individual acts, or incomplete knowledge of them. Since it is impossible to know anyone completely, it would seem advisable not to judge at all.

A lot of people are uncomfortable visiting cemeteries, because they only associate them with loss, grief and tears; I think it is good to remember that those tears of loss are also tears of love.

My husband and I took a trip for our 25th wedding anniversary (nearly twenty years ago) to visit some historic sites in the Northeast part of the country. One of the places we went was the Civil War battlefield, at

Gettysburg, Penn. It wouldn't have been my first choice, but I knew my husband really wanted to go there. He is a former Civil War Re-enactor, a lover of history and a collector of Civil War items and books. I was worried that the sense of suffering and death would be so strong there that I would be overwhelmed by it. The more I came to know about the Civil War, through my husband's study of it, the more senseless and inhumane I found it. I feel that way about war in general, and I would like to point out that re-enactors by and large are not glorifying war, but studying it from many perspectives in order to understand why it happened, and what steps could have been taken to prevent it. My preconceived notion of Gettysburg could not have been more wrong.

Once we got past the museums and other touristy parts of the site, I was instantly overwhelmed, not by the spectre of death, but by the amazing peace and serenity of the battlefield itself. How is it possible for a place of death and carnage on such a large scale, to be peaceful and serene?

Abraham Lincoln, in his famous Gettysburg Address, spoke of the battlefield having been consecrated by those who fought, and those who died there. The word consecrated is closely related to the word 'hallowed" and hallowed means "to make holy". It isn't death that makes Gettysburg "hallowed ground", it's the act of sacrifice. The peace and serenity there, is an act of God, who cleanses away the agony and torment of death, and replaces it with heavenly consecration. You can feel the presence of God so clearly, in that place of otherworldly stillness; I could have stayed there forever.

"Nothing can make up for the absence of someone whom we love, and it would be wrong to try to find a substitute; we must simply hold out and see it through. That sounds very hard at first, but at the same time, it's a great consolation, for the gap, as long as it remains unfilled, preserves the bonds between us. It is nonsense to say that God fills the gap; God doesn't fill it, but on the contrary, keeps it empty, and so helps us to keep our former communion with each other, even at the cost of pain."

Dietrick Bonhoeffer
Lutheran Theologian
Executed by the Nazis

WAITING FOR THE SUN TO SHINE

I was a child of the 50's, a teenager in the 60's and a young adult wife and mother in the 70's. As a teenager, I was mature in a lot of ways, some of which nearly drove my parent's crazy. I was always a person who spent a lot of time deep in thought. Sometimes, I was creating things in my mind. My teachers wrote on the back of every report card they ever issued, that I spent too much time daydreaming. I wasn't good at thinking about what other people wanted me to focus on. Sometimes, I was trying to figure out where I had come from, why I was here and what I was supposed to do with my life.

By the time I was 16 yrs. old, I decided I had become the person I was destined to be for the duration of my life. That idea was anything but mature! In the 60's or 70's (can't remember exactly), there was a popular saying that made its way on to everything from coffee cups to bumper stickers; *"Be patient; God isn't finished with me yet."* If only I'd gotten the point; I'm sure it would have changed my life. Had I realized that God would never be "finished" with me and that to be alive is to change continually, it might have impacted many of the decisions I made… or, maybe not?

It's now 2019, and as I look back at my life's experiences, I see many roses (good times) and a few thorns (times of confusion, pain and loss), but would I change any of it if I could? I rather think not. All of my life's experiences have brought me to this point, this place, this peace. I believe each decision, dilemma, mistake, fork in the road, joy, and heartache were mine to experience. If I were to change even one thing, would I be who I am in this moment? The most obvious answer is no. Would I have chosen the grief I have experienced through the loss of my

son Ethan, at the hands of another? No, that wouldn't have been my choice and I don't believe
It was God's choice either. I believe God knew it would happen, but he didn't make it happen. If the next question is *"Well, He could have stopped it, couldn't He?"* In the truth my spirit has come to know through the tragedy of losing Ethan, God doesn't interfere in our lives that way. He takes the bad things we experience and makes as much good come from them as He can, if we will allow it. I also know God doesn't believe dying is the worst thing that could happen to you. I know God grieves when a life is ended prematurely, and in a manner unnatural to the universal laws. God is not indifferent to our pain and loss. If that had been the case, I wouldn't have survived the most painful experience of my life. Instead, through God's love and compassion, He has created an alternative or parallel life for me. A life I am able to live in peace and gratitude, for all I've been given. Instead, God through His Son and the Holy Spirit has allowed me to feel my son's spirit close to me whenever I focus on him and has allowed me to hear my son's voice and thoughts, hundreds of times. I am still astonished at the magnitude of God's gifts to me.

God is still "not finished" with me yet, nor is He finished with my son or any other spirit living in this world or the next. God will still be creating when time in this world has ended. God has always been and always will be. We will always be continuing to become what He created us to be. What greater reason for hope could there be?

UNTIL THE TWELFTH OF NEVER

You ask how long I'll love you?
Oh, how can I explain?
That I will love you always,
Through joy and deepest pain.

For love has no beginning,
And surely has no end.
For love is everlasting,
As sacred as the rain.

Love is pure and love is sweet,
As the fragrance of a rose.
As brilliant as the setting sun,
That brings the day to close.

Love is just the stuff of life;
What matters, anyhow.
Love exists, within the past,
As surely as does it now.

Love is what the soul doth crave,
As nourishing as the rain,
That falls upon the dust of earth,
To replenish the barren plain.

Love is like the air we breathe,
So vital to our lives
And when once born, can never die,
So, endlessly survives.

Just as God your spirit knew,
Before your time was wound.
I loved you, though I didn't know,
My love would know no bound.

If I loved you then and I love you now,
How could it then be said;
The love I had could come full-stop,
Because they call you dead?

The light of God in you was placed,
Before He gave you breath,
The light of Spirit still doth shine,
It knows no earthly death.

Spirit of Truth to me revealed,
He wrote it on my heart,
That love, as you, can never die;
And from me never part
                                    J.S. Schmidt

So many amazing things have happened in my life, in the span of time since the passing of my son. One of the most amazing, is the fact that all of these things occurred, after I thought my life was virtually over. When Ethan's life was taken, I agreed to go on living, but I expected to walk through life sad and empty until it was over; I thought I would never know joy or peace again. I was so wrong! I was wrong about so many things! It's hard to know where to begin to explain what has happened to me these past four years. I guess I'll just start at the beginning...

The worst day of my entire life, was the day Ethan was murdered. I don't think I'll ever get used to saying that. The second worst day was when I sat beside his casket at the cemetery, knowing that in minutes, I would have to leave him there and walk away. In my heart, I knew he wasn't really there in that casket; I knew his spirit lived in another place. In those awful moments a miracle occurred that changed my life forever. The following excerpt from "Learn to be Still" explains what happened that day...

The event I want to relate took place on the day of the service that celebrated Ethan's life, Sept. 19, 2015.

At the conclusion of the service, we went out to get into our vehicles for the short trip to the cemetery, less than a mile from the high school where the service was held. I have only vague memories of the drive, but I remember getting out of the car and walking to where the canopy and chairs were waiting for our arrival. I sat down and the graveside service began shortly afterward. I was seated near the center of the first row of chairs. If I looked straight ahead, all I could see was the casket that held my precious son, so I preferred to look down at the flowers that had been placed around the base it was resting on. I don't remember the prayers, or the scripture that was read. I remember the sound of the bagpipes. Ethan loved them and had offered to arrange for a piper to play at the burial of my father, which didn't take place for months after his own. Soon, those in attendance began to file through in front of us to offer hugs and words of support. I have no concept of the number of people who had come with us to the cemetery, but it seemed to me there were many. If I looked to the right or the left, all I saw were people. At one point, there was a slight break in the flow of well-wishers and I took a moment to center myself and take a long, deep breath. As I did so, I looked to my right beyond the canopy and then quickly back down at the flowers. I quickly looked back, at someone I thought I recognized as a friend of nearly forty years; someone whose life I entered at a time of tragic loss for him. The bond that was forged in that time of trial for him, is strong and almost sacred. I would never wish to lose his friendship or respect, but what happened in the moment I looked back at him was unbelievably profound and I'm sure he's totally unaware of it. The first draft of this chapter revealed not only his name, but the terrible tragedy that precipitated our friendship. He is not "in his heart", (so he says) a religious person. Because of what I'm about to relate, I have chosen to keep his identity to myself in order to protect his privacy and his personal beliefs.

As I saw him standing there in the cemetery that day, the thing that drew my attention, was that he was the only person in that frame. That seemed odd, as if you looked in any other direction, you would have seen groups or clusters of people filling every space. As I reflected on that thought, he raised his head and looked directly into my eyes. My friend has blue-grey eyes, but the eyes I was looking into were very dark brown and I realized, it wasn't my friend's face I saw. The dark eyes were fiercely compassionate and the intensity of love and empathy they projected was unnerving. Behind the eyes, there was this sense of carefully controlled energy—power, if you will, like nuclear energy, the sheer force of which, (if unleashed) could be cataclysmic. I knew I was seeing something spiritual—a transfiguration of some kind. As with all of the spiritual communications I have experienced, what I heard was telepathic in nature. The message was, *"I'm here, I've always been here."* Then the image nodded toward the casket and said, *"I have him. He's with me, and he's just fine, so don't worry about him."* My first thoughts were that it must have been an angel, but as time passed, I knew that wasn't quite right. The alternative to that thought, I tried for six months to dismiss from my mind, because it seemed beyond rationality. Finally, I could deny it no longer, I was looking into the eyes of Jesus. I am still overwhelmed by that thought, but the truth of it will not be denied.

On the day my son's life was taken, the world as I knew it was destroyed—wiped away as though a tornado had cleared everything away that I knew to be so. It was probably weeks and perhaps even months before I began to see things in my mind with any clarity. Most of us have seen pictures of the aftermath of tornadoes where the only thing left is bare slabs, where homes and lives once stood. On the bare slab I saw before me, stood only the truth. It was so easy to see once everything else had been removed. That truth stands firm: it will not be swayed and it will not fade or waiver. In this new life that I live, I sometimes see the truth standing in the center of that slab as a large cross that glows in the darkness, like a star shines on a dark night. Truth is truth, but it may appear differently to each of us. This is my image of truth.

On that day at the cemetery, as I looked into those dark eyes, not knowing if I should try to look away or continue to meet that piercing gaze in the face I saw, that was not my friend's, I tried to memorize some of the details because I knew I wouldn't be able to remember them clearly. The complexion was lighter than the artist depictions of Christ one is accustomed to seeing. The jaw line and chin were squared or rather sharp. The face was definitely masculine. The hair was dark chestnut brown, but with a hint of red. The eyebrows were heavy and darker than the hair color. There was no beard.

After what seemed like several minutes locked in that compassionate gaze, someone stepped in front of me and I was forced to look away. When I looked back, I saw only my friend, as I had always known him.

I don't believe this happened to me because I'm special in any sense. I believe it happened because one night as I experienced pain of such magnitude, I thought I couldn't survive it, I knocked on heaven's door and asked for help and comfort and I received what was promised.

When Jesus said to me," *I'm here, I've always been here."* It changed my life. Those are the 6 most important words my ears have ever heard. In that moment, I was so relieved and grateful, but in the same moment, it made me so sad, because until then I didn't know Jesus was less than 10 feet away. I didn't know I could have run to His embrace at any moment of my life. I know it now and I have done it many times and I can only say there is no greater comfort to be found!

I was baptized as a follower of Christ, at the age of twelve. I knew Jesus loved me. I was told to ask Him to come into my heart, but until that moment in the cemetery, I never felt Him there. I had neglected somehow, all those years, to create a real relationship with Him.

Jesus has held my hand in each and every step I've taken out of the valley of the shadow of death. During the time I was editing this book, I had another revelation about this particular experience. I was thinking about how difficult it was to try to relate to others how different Jesus appeared from every other human being I have ever seen. As I was having that thought; which I have had numerous times in the four years since I saw Jesus, on the day we buried our son; these words suddenly popped into my mind: "Shroud of Turin". The shroud of Turin is a fascinating artifact that many believe to be an image of the crucified Christ, that somehow became emblazoned on the piece of linen, that covered his body in the tomb. Many scientific tests have been conducted on it over the years. As technology presents newer avenues of dating materials etc., more tests are conducted. The artifact is in the possession of the catholic church and is currently housed in the Cathedral of Saint John the Baptist, in Turin, Italy. Most of the tests have been inconclusive. The carbon dating tests initially indicated the shroud fabric was from the Medieval period, but that conclusion has since been re-examined, and is considered not conclusive also. Having given you a brief history of the shroud, let me say that after hearing those words in my mind recently, I looked at online pictures of the shroud, and the image much more closely resembles the Jesus I saw, on that day at the cemetery. I believe Jesus can appear however He chooses at any given time; this is what I recall, from my own experience.

This is the place in Prairie Lawn Cemetery, Peabody Ks. Where Ethan's earthly remains now rest. About 10-12ft. from this spot is where I saw Jesus on the day of Ethan's graveside service.

LISTEN TO THE MUSIC

The musical messages I receive from Ethan began on Thursday Sept. 17, 2015—three days after he departed this physical life. I was riding in the van that Ethan and Liz owned, returning to our home in Kansas to prepare for Ethan's service, which was scheduled for Saturday. Tom was driving and my grandson, Connor, was in the front passenger seat. They were listening to Pandora on satellite radio; it was a station Ethan had created for himself; and all of the songs were painfully familiar to me. Pandora was a relatively new thing in my world and I didn't exactly understand the process. Ethan had set up a Pandora station for me at Christmas (2014); He explained that you could develop or personalize your station by accepting or rejecting the music that was being randomly played, with the computer system driving the selection of music.

It is hard to recall all of the songs I heard that day or the order in which they were played, but they changed my life forever as they brought me back from the void of hopelessness.

As I listened to the songs, I heard Ethan speak to me, he said," *Mom, It's really me, Ethan. I'm trying to talk to you through this music. I'm here! I exist.* That is how the communication I have with Ethan began; it has continued for nearly five years. It has become easier as I have learned how to listen for it and also how I can initiate it. When I began to write LTBS, my sister said, *"Don't you think it will make other people feel bad to know that you hear Ethan's voice and they haven't had that experience with the child they lost?* I have thought about that many times and I'm sure it sometimes happens, but I know I'm supposed to share the knowledge that this is possible. People don't try to find something if they don't believe it exists. I have wondered many times why this happens to me. The only answer I can find is that God knew I needed it to survive losing Ethan and I think he wanted me to experience it and then articulate it in a way that others might understand and accept. I have a very deep sense of peace about it, even though, I know the last thing I would want to do is hurt someone who is already hurting so badly. I pray every time I present this story or hand someone a book, that God will not let the things I say, cause someone to walk away from Him in disbelief. I pray He will never allow me to harm anyone by sharing this information. When I had doubts early on about whether this was real, Ethan said to me," *I know you sometimes think about the night you arrived in Cleveland (Miss.) and you were so devastated and lost. You asked God to help and comfort you. God would not answer your request with some kind of trick, when you were sincerely begging for His help. That should be proof that this is real and comes from the Light.*"

GIVE ONE HEART

When you begin to walk the valley of grief, particularly the sudden, explosive, disorienting kind of grief that accompanies something such as a murder; you start to see some striking paradoxes. One of the first I noticed in my own life, was the feeling of extreme weakness and unexplained strength, which seemed to exist in the same moments. The only way I believe it's possible to account for this mysterious surge of strength, in a moment of near total weakness, is that this is where God has stepped into your life and sent His angels of love and protection to assist you.

"For He shall give His angels charge over you. To keep you in all of your ways."

Psalm 91:11

When you have lost someone as precious as your child, it is hard to imagine how it will be possible to go on with your life. How will you ever smile or laugh again? Where could you possibly find joy or peace? You can't even imagine that blessings, of any kind, could come to you through such a devastating loss; but they are there and in surprising number.

In the midst of grief, you are so totally focused on loss, it is at first, very difficult to see how there could possibly be anything gained. The gains are not instead of your loss, but in spite of it.

When my son's life was taken, I was so devastated I had little will to go on living. It just seemed too painful and too difficult. I promised God I wouldn't do anything to end my earthly life, but I also believed my joy in that life was completely gone. I expected to merely exist until God decided my life was over. God just wasn't going to accept that!

"You will show me the path of life; in Your presence is fullness of joy."

Psalm 16:11

One morning, early in Spring, the year following Ethan's passing, I sat outside my back door on a garden bench with my granddaughter, Brianna. Ethan's family had come to visit for Spring Break, the sun was shining brightly and the sky was clear and blue. It was a lovely day, but my heart felt empty and sad. I looked around the back yard at the many flower beds and empty pots. At any other time, I would have been anxious to fill them with flowers and I would have been looking forward to watering and nurturing them through the hot Kansas summer. On that day, I wondered if I would even bother to plant anything. Nothing seemed to have the same meaning for me, since Ethan had left this world. As I sat there feeling so low and dejected; I suddenly saw the tiniest white butterfly floating and dipping and diving right in front of me and amazingly, in that moment, I felt joy. It was only a moment, but it was proof that joy was still a possibility. In grief, progress usually comes in very small steps, that over time create big changes, that gently propel you forward.

I was 64 years old when Ethan was taken. Almost from my earliest conscious moments, I had been afraid of death; terrified would be a more accurate word. It wasn't as if I didn't believe in God or an afterlife, but like most people, I feared the transition into something unknown. I've read that many people aren't afraid of dying, they are afraid of being in pain or fear during their last moments and I believe we all dread the inevitable separation from those we love.

Over the years, as I began to experience the loss of grandparents, aunts and uncles etc. my fears only multiplied as I witnessed the intense grief of my parents and other relatives. My fear became more like a phobia. When I was in my early 30's, I experienced the death of a friend who died in her sleep, at the age of 29. There were multiple attempts to find the cause of her passing, but all that could be determined was that her heart had stopped, with no discernable cause. I was so sad and shocked, but also terrified that you could just go to sleep at such a young age and not wake up. I began to be afraid to go to sleep and I started to have panic attacks that were so frequent and severe, I was put on medication to try to control them. The medication only made me feel as if everything was moving in slow motion and I felt drugged and foggy.

One day, as I sat in church, I heard the pastor say," *if you are suffering any affliction, pain or fear, ask God to remove it from you and if you truly believe; He will take it from you.*" I had tried everything else anyone had suggested, so I thought "*Well, it couldn't hurt.*" The attacks didn't mysteriously appear all at once. They would continue to cripple me with unreasonable and unexplained panic, but I would simply say to them: "*No, you don't exist anymore and I refuse to acknowledge you!*" In fairly short order they were gone and have never bothered me again.

"I sought the Lord, and He heard me and delivered me from all my fears."
Psalm 34:4

A couple of years after my son's passing, I was driving to a dental appointment in a nearby city, and I passed a place where someone was obviously injured while working. There was an ambulance pulled to the side of the street with lights flashing. I saw a lift with a bucket that was elevated and very close to an overhead powerline. There were co-workers in hard hats standing close by, who looked anxious and frightened. My middle son, Jeff is an electric lineman in another city, so this scene took on a more personal aspect than it might otherwise have done.

My thoughts immediately went to the injured worker; was he seriously injured or worse, had this accident taken his life? Was another mother or wife about to receive an awful phone call, similar to the one I received from my daughter-in-law on the day Ethan's life was senselessly taken? I can't bear to think of anyone else experiencing that unbearable anguish, yet I know it happens every day, in hundreds of places. As I passed the scene of the accident on that day, I began to tremble and cry and it was hard to pull myself together enough to go to my appointment, but I made it through. I cried all the way home and struggled with those intense feelings for a couple of days. It wasn't a full-blown panic; it was more like the kind of flashbacks you experience with PTSD.

These days, when something disturbs my spirit's peace like that, I know to go to God as soon as possible, to find renewed comfort and strength. The paradox that encompasses this whole story is that through the horrible experience of losing my son, I no longer have a debilitating fear of death. What disturbs me now is the suffering it causes in this world. I have learned that death isn't what I imagined it to be. Logic would tell you that the experience of losing someone so precious, should intensify your fear of death, but my experience has been anything but logical and my fear has all but dissipated.

"Darkness is powerless before the onslaught of light, and so it is with death. We have allowed ourselves to think of it as a dark door, when actually it is a rainbow bridge, spanning the gulf between two worlds."
Dr. Norman Vincent Peale

Let me say, following Dr. Peale's quote; If you are a person who may be now or have ever been or may be in the future, contemplating taking your own life; PLEASE! I beg you, give God a chance to help you. All you need do is ask from the depth of your soul and believe that with God all things are possible! Then wait; the help you seek probably won't come in a flash of lightning, but it will surely come.

Perhaps, the most profoundly emotional paradox I have experienced, occurred in the moments I realized Jesus was standing about ten feet away from me, as I sat beside the casket that held my son. It was near the close of the graveside service, when I looked up and thought I recognized an old friend, who has suffered two very sudden and tragic losses in his own life. It was him, but not him at the same time. The eyes that met mine were the eyes of Jesus. I don't know how that happened, but I know why it happened; it was what I needed to survive. God has given me everything I needed to go on living. He gives what is needed, when it is needed. If you think about all I lost on the day Ethan's life ended, you must ask yourself how it is possible for me to say *"My life is richly and abundantly blessed!"*

Jesus looked at them and said "With man this is impossible, but with God all things are possible."

Mathew 19:26

THE RIVER OF TEARS

The river of tears;
That flows from my heart;
The torrent that rages;
Where I've been torn apart.

Like rapids it dashes;
As it runs through the peaks;
Through the valleys and lower;
To the depths that it seeks.

It creates a new channel;
As it cuts like a knife;
Shaping and curving;
As it forms a new life.

As it flows down the mountain;
It's ferocity wains;
It slows its pursuit;
As it reaches the plains.

Its anger subsiding;
A gentle brook it became;
The river has changed me;
I'm no longer the same.

Its crashing and dashing;
Its raging all gone;
The water is still;
In the light of the dawn.

The river of tears;
Now seldom it spills;
Down the side of the mountain;
To the low rolling hills.

Its task was to change me;
To calm and to heal;
To give me new life;
That no torrent can steal.

It lies in a pool now;
Beneath the great mountain;
Its surface like glass;
Till it flows from the fountain.

In the midst of the pool;
Sits an angel of white;
From its trumpet now flowing;
Tears of pain turned to light.

J.S. Schmidt- Mar. 12, 2020

After Ethan's passing in 2015, it was quickly decided that Ethan's wife and the kids would return to Mississippi to finish out the school year, which had barely begun at the time of the tragic event. When Liz could get a teaching position near Lawrence, she and the kids would return to Kansas to live.

Before going to Lubbock to take a position in the History Dept. at Texas Tech, Ethan and Liz and their two young sons lived in Eudora, Ks. It's a small town very close to Kansas University, where Ethan received his Ph.D. Our middle son and his family, have lived in Eudora for many years. It seemed natural for Liz and the kids, now including a daughter, to move back to a familiar location and close to family, so she would have help when it was needed. I'm sure she would want me to say that the people of Cleveland, Miss., particularly her teacher friends and Ethan's colleagues, as well as the people from their church, were very supportive of her and the kids during those first incredibly tough months of trying to live with Ethan absent from their lives. Over Spring Break in 2016, Liz learned she had been accepted to teach at an elementary school in Lawrence. She bought a house in Eudora and they prepared to move, when the school year ended.

Tom and I knew we wanted to move to be close to them and help in any way we could. We had a home that we loved, in a place that we had called home for our entire 41 yr. marriage; I had grown up there. Three generations of my family graduated from the high school there. For most of my life, I had never given a thought to leaving my hometown. It was about 2-1/2 hours away from Eudora and we knew we needed to be much closer if we were to be available to help Liz. I began looking for a place for us, even though Tom wasn't ready to move, for a variety of reasons. I wanted to be there when Ethan's family arrived.

The house we had lived in for 16 yrs. prior to this time, was a large Queen Anne Victorian. It was our dream home. We loved it and I always believed it would be traumatic for me to have to leave it when the time came, but that all changed in an instant, when Ethan's life was taken.

When I began to think about our next home, I knew it needed to be a place we could transition to as easily as possible. We were deeply embedded in grief and we had already experienced tremendous change to our lives, by the act of a person who didn't even know us.

I was surprised when the idea of living in a parsonage first surfaced in my mind. The thought had never occurred to me before. Parsonages, were places where a minister lived while serving a specific church. It was usually property that was owned by the church and the minister could live there rent free. Many churches no longer provide a parsonage for their minister and his family. It wasn't long before the idea of living in a parsonage was deeply rooted in my heart, as well as my mind and spirit. I knew I was looking for a sanctuary, a quiet place that would help me find a way to rebuild my life.

In the early hours of my grief, I turned to God for help to bear what then seemed unbearable. Heavenly comfort and guidance, was mine within hours of making my desperate plea to God.

The only direction I had regarding a house, was that it needed to be a former parsonage (most are no longer used for that purpose). It needed to be an older home and it needed to be smaller than the house we were in. I knew I didn't have the strength or the desire to care for a large home, going forward. I began to look for something that would meet our needs, in the general area we would be moving to. There were mostly new homes available there and all of our home furnishings were antiques and while you could put them in a newer home, they really belong to another time.

I set my sights on a two -story home that had been the parsonage for the local Church of Christ. I thought it was big enough to allow us to keep most of the furniture we had, but small enough for us to care for going forward. I set up an appointment with the realtor, whose name was on the sign in the yard. After seeing inside, I decided it would work well enough and began the task of selling my husband on the idea. He was still working as the office administrator for the heating and air conditioning company he had been with for nearly twenty-five years and he was still several years away from retirement age. His place of employment was 2-1/2 hours away from the house I wanted him to buy and he was still paying for the house we were in; these were large hurdles to get over. It was only months since we had lost our son and we were both really struggling to find our balance; life seemed uncertain and the future unfathomable. Tom was understandably reluctant, but I knew I needed to be close by, when Liz and the kids moved into their new home, without Ethan.

I looked at the big white house several times before I convinced Tom to come with me. He thought it would work, but he wasn't overwhelmed with the idea and he still thought it was too soon, for all of the reasons I've mentioned.

After we left the house that day, we drove to the next street over, (Church Street) and there was a house for sale. We later learned the sign had only been in the front yard for 30 minutes, when we saw it. The house was a Queen

Anne Cottage, the same style, in a smaller version, of the house we were living in. I was shocked when the owner said, *"This used to be the Methodist parsonage."* I looked at the house that same day and loved it immediately, but I still had to convince Tom to sail over those hurdles. Our son, Jeff's family looked at both of the houses with us and they overwhelming liked the Queen Anne. Tom liked the house, but still didn't see how we could buy it since we had no idea how long it would take to sell the big Victorian. He just kept saying, *"We just can't buy a house now!"*

Later that same day, Tom and I were on the way to visit his mother and we talked about the house as we drove to her apartment. In one breath, the same sentence, he went from saying, *"There's no way I can do this, to suddenly saying, "I know what I can do!! I can do this and this, and this!!!"* It was one of the strangest things I've ever seen; I know it had to be the Holy Spirit's intervention. We were led to the perfect house and even though there were a few obstacles to get by, it worked out beautifully. The first time my sister-in-law, Cristy, saw the house after we were settled in it, she said, *"You shrunk your house! This is your house!!"*

Tom was able to retire early and has since painted the house in nearly identical fashion to the big Victorian and he has filled many of the windows with beautiful stained-glass pieces; he loved and missed the stained glass from our former home. I see these beautiful windows every morning when I open my eyes and it sometimes feels like I fell asleep in a church. It's a comforting thought. The parsonage has become both a home that embraces me and a sanctuary for me, as I continue to heal from tremendous loss and strive to move closer to God.

THE VESSEL

The vessel; alone it stands;
Without shape; devoid of form;
Unknown to the potter's hands;
Until in darkness, amid the storm;
The potter spins the wheel, in love;
Creating the image from his heart;
Angels guiding him, from above;
A masterpiece now stands apart.

J.S. Schmidt- May 21, 2018

GREAT IS THY FAITHFULNESS

As children, many of us learned to reveal hidden pictures by drawing a line between a pattern of dots on a piece of paper. Dot-to-dot books have been a popular amusement for young children for many years and are still available, even in the age of technology we are living through. It's a very simple process and one we can and should use in our lives to assess where we have been, where we are, and where we are headed, in our journey of life. It is so important to learn to recognize patterns as we navigate the ups and downs of our lives. If we use the example of heavenly constellations, we can see they are made up of various configurations of stars(dots). What makes them recognizable to us, are the patterns or placements of the individual stars, that distinguish them from the other trillions of stars in the night sky. Their patterns become even clearer when we mentally or physically draw lines between each star (connect the dots).

In our busy lives, most of us seldom take the time to look back at where we started on our journey. We have a tendency to look at life as a linear process; we are born, we attend school, we attend college, we get a job, many of us marry and have children, we become grandparents, we retire; if we are fortunate we have some time to do all of the things we enjoy, that we didn't have time for while we were working and raising our children and then life here comes to its conclusion.

There was a popular song years ago, titled, "Is That All There Is?" One day about seven years ago, I asked myself that question. I had just celebrated my 60th birthday. My family threw a surprise birthday party for me, which I enjoyed very much. I went home and went to bed and when I woke up the next morning; it was as if someone had turned my world completely around. It was a very sudden change in nearly everything. I began to look at where I was at that time in my life and I asked myself, *"What lies ahead for me? Have I done everything in my life I was meant to do?"*

From the time I was about seven years old, my only dream or goal for my life was to be a mother. That was my own goal, it wasn't something I was pushed into: it was what I wanted. I achieved that goal just before my 18th birthday. I was privileged to become a mother 3 times. I wasn't the perfect mother I envisioned, but it became the most meaningful and fulfilling experience of my life; nothing else would have meaning in my life if I were to remove that experience.

God, through the Holy Spirit has revealed many things to me in the years since I lost my son, Ethan. It's as if He's slowly filling in the blanks, in the story of my life. Sometimes, it's truth that I learn and sometimes, the Spirit takes me back to my youth and gives me a new perspective on the things that occurred, by revealing why they happened as they did. Each time this happens, I learn something and I am able to see the events with much more clarity than ever before. It helps me understand myself at a deeper level and it reveals God's presence and intercession in my life, in ways I didn't see at the time the events took place. Only quite recently, I was thinking about being a young girl and begging God to allow me to have children of my own, when the time was right for that to happen. Suddenly, a number of seemingly unrelated things began to form a narrative I'd never been aware of before.

On the morning after my 60th birthday, my children had all grown up, they were married, I was a grandmother of 5 and I had been happily married to my husband, Tom, for 37 years. I was content, my life was good, but my question was; *"Is that all there is? Is there something else I'm supposed to do?"*

After raising my children, I found myself with lots of time on my hands. I had been mostly a stay-at-home mom, but I had worked intermittently at various things. Usually, I did things that allowed me to work from home, or to be home when my children were out of school. After Ethan went to college, I also began to volunteer in our church and community. I was fundraising chairman for our church. I was director of a community quilt project where volunteers made quilts and we auctioned them and gave money to various organizations in town. I was president of our Main Street organization, which functioned somewhat like a Chamber of Commerce. My husband and I directed a project of volunteers who cared for the city flowerbeds, in the parks and public areas of our little town. For a while, I owned a fabric shop and then a flower shop; I was a professional seamstress for many years. I did a lot of things before that day immediately following my 60th birthday, when I woke up to a new world.

There was nothing I could attribute this sudden and amazing change to. I knew where I was and where I had been, but when I tried to see where the future might take me, all I saw was a fog. The one thing that was clear on that day, was that I needed to get out of all of the things I was doing to keep myself busy and spend time just "being" and feeding my spirit.

I did just that for the next four years. Then on Sept. 14, 2015, I received the phone call that changed my life forever. My son Ethan, my youngest, had been murdered by one of his colleagues. What was most precious to me, my child, was taken away that day and my life could never be the same.

I read recently, that when we are faced with unspeakable tragedy or grief, we have the choice to be "bitter or to be better"; I chose better. It was a clear and conscious choice and I remember the moment the decision was made. It has been a long and painful journey from that day to this one. Only God could have taken me from that place of darkness and hopelessness to this day, when I stand here in gratitude and wholeness of spirit. As I look back many years over the course of my life, I can see many dots, many points at which God was leading me to a better place. I believe we could all find spiritual peace and wholeness easier and faster if we learned to recognize and connect the dots in our lives sooner. There were so many years God was working to help me, when I wasn't even aware that He was there. I have that awareness now, so clearly, and I know He's present in my life every moment, especially in the worst moments. As the words of that beautiful old hymn say," Great is Thy Faithfulness"!

THANK YOU, LORD

This morning brought the first day of August, 2018; nearly 3 years have passed since Ethan was taken from us. As the anniversary date draws close each year, I struggle with emotions I have learned to keep balanced the majority of the time. I still have tough days, but they are much farther apart and the recovery seems to come faster than it did at first. There are still tears nearly every day, at some point. Sometimes, they are brief and easily brushed away; sometimes they go on for hours and won't recede until they are totally spent. They often come out of nowhere and when there is no identifiable reason for them to appear. At times, I have been astonished at how many tears one person could produce. At some point, they became tears of healing, but even now, they are sometimes, tears of longing for my son's physical presence. I feel his spiritual presence every day and it is such an incredible blessing. There are times when I feel guilty for having such a comfort, that I know so many are without. I want people to know this is possible in their lives too. That is part of the reason I have written about the most personal and painful experience of my life; I want to help people. I want to give comfort to other people, because I know too well the pain they are experiencing. Writing is my effort to bless others, in my small way, because I have been blessed in ways I could not have imagined.

The past twenty-four hours have been a time of heightened emotion for me. This was triggered by a movie I attended yesterday, with most of the female members of my family. It was one of those just-for-fun movies, with great music, great scenery, lots of laughs and a few tears; at least, that's what I thought it would be.

There's a scene in the movie where a young (college age) girl gives birth. She is unmarried and estranged from her family. Except for the kindness of a stranger, she is all alone. I've always loved babies and the births of my own three children were the happiest, most hopeful moments of my life. But then, my son's life was taken and every baby I see reminds me of what I lost, on that terrible day. I began to cry in the theater; I managed to make a hasty departure after the film and cried all the way home.

I cried for about an hour after I got home and then suddenly, it stopped. This morning, I was still a little down from the movie experience, but otherwise, I was having a normal day. In the late afternoon, I sat down to rest and thought I might take a short nap. I began to think about how far I've come in these three years since that tragic day and how far God has brought me back, from the utter desolation of that loss. I was suddenly overwhelmed with the gratitude I thought I had adequately expressed, on more than one occasion. I began to weep uncontrollably and it didn't stop for over two hours.

God has used all of the known aspects of heaven to rebuild my life; Jesus, The Holy Spirit, angels, the saints (those I love, who have passed to eternity). I have been given everything I needed at the exact time and in the precise measure I needed, to be able to heal and find balance and peace.

It wasn't in God's plan to restore the life I had, which would have meant restoring my son's wounded body, to life on earth. My son is healed in heaven and God has chosen to give me an alternative life; almost a parallel life, to the one I had. I couldn't live that broken life with joy and peace, the life God has replaced it with is very similar, but enough different that it's possible for me to go on and be happy. My son is still gone physically from my life, but

167

the gift of having his spirit with me every day makes that absence bearable.

It feels as if God himself has plucked me from the middle of the ocean, or pulled me back from the edge of a cliff. I felt so destroyed, but God was watching and He wouldn't let me go. His love is all-consuming and so pure, it's impossible to feel anything close to the depth of it and not weep in gratitude.

The song that is the title of this chapter ("Thank You, Lord, for your blessings on me") is from the Southern Gospel genre. Until I lost my son, I had never listened to Southern Gospel, or any kind of gospel music, for that matter. It was something I just felt myself drawn to, for absolutely no reason that I can explain. I found much comfort in it and still listen to it regularly. This song, is about being grateful to God for all you've been given; the roof over your head, the food on your table, a bed to sleep in, your family, life itself.

Of all the gifts God has given me in my season of grief, I am most amazed by the gifts of joy and gratitude. Those were feelings I never believed it would be possible for me to experience again, here on earth. They continually point out to me that God makes the impossible, possible every day, for millions of people. I believed my joy had been stolen from me, when my son was murdered, because I believed my family was where my joy originated. As the Holy Spirit worked to heal my spirit, I was surprised to experience joy in some very insignificant things. I learned that our joy comes from relationship with God and as this scripture attests, joy is the fruit of the Spirit.

"but the fruit of the Spirit is love, JOY, peace, longsuffering, kindness, goodness, faithfulness, gentleness, self-control. "
Galatians 5:22,23

168

One day in early June of 2016, about 9 months after our son's life was taken, my sister and I were wandering through a little second-hand shop, that was operated by a local church. I had little interest in buying anything, but I was just looking around because my sister always enjoys going there. At that point in time, I had very little interest in anything. As I wandered along, I looked up and about twenty feet in front of where I stood was something that literally made me gasp in delight...

At this point, I have to stop and give you some background, or you won't understand my reaction at all. Most of that initial year of grief, my emotions seemed almost dead. I could cry, and I did every day. Sometimes I cried all day long! I couldn't and still don't feel anger, I rarely laughed, though I tried to smile, mostly for the benefit of others. I didn't care about any of my lifelong interests or hobbies, which included my flower gardens, holiday decorating, sewing, quilting etc.

I used to tell people that I loved sewing so much that every day I got to sew was a good day. It was three years, after Ethan's passing, before I touched my sewing machine. I was a professional seamstress for many years and made nearly everything that can be made from fabric. Of all of the things I made over the long span of years since I began sewing (50 years ago), the thing I loved most was wedding gowns. I wanted to make wedding gowns so much that I was almost willing to pay my customers to let me make them a dress. I eventually stopped making them because I realized I was working for about 50 cents an hour. These are often very difficult dresses and very labor intensive. The gowns I made were heirloom quality fabrics and each part of them was made to the very best standards I could produce. My dream for them was that one day, many years after the wedding day, they would be pulled out of the box or trunk they were stored in and be even more beautiful with age. I have always felt that weddings are one of the most hopeful experiences that human beings celebrate. After losing Ethan, I felt more hopeless than at any time of my life, but when I asked God to help me make it through those awful days, I knew were ahead of me, He began to restore my hope and my joy. So now, back to the story in the second-hand shop...

Hanging on a display, right in the middle of the aisle, were three absolutely adorable wedding gowns. Over the years, I have amassed a modest collection of wedding gowns. When I see one that is unusual or from an era that isn't represented in my collection, I try to purchase it. Some of them are ridiculously priced and it would have to be a magnificent gown in order for me to break the price point I think is reasonable. All three of the dresses on the display in front of me, were $20 or less. I really loved them all and just seeing them lifted my spirits, but at first, I didn't think about buying them; the longer I stood there, I began to consider it. I decided it would be foolish to buy them because I was moving and trying to get rid of unnecessary things. At one time, I was doing fashion shows and really believed at some point I would do a vintage wedding gown show, but then we lost Ethan and life changed so much I couldn't see myself ever doing those things again. I admired the three dresses, but left the store without them. Before we had driven four or five blocks from the store, something clearly told me to go back and buy the dresses. The reaction I had of joy and hope was so strong and so foreign to me at that time, I just knew it was meant to be.

God has all kinds of lovely surprises instore for us, but we have to be paying attention in order to receive these surprise blessings.

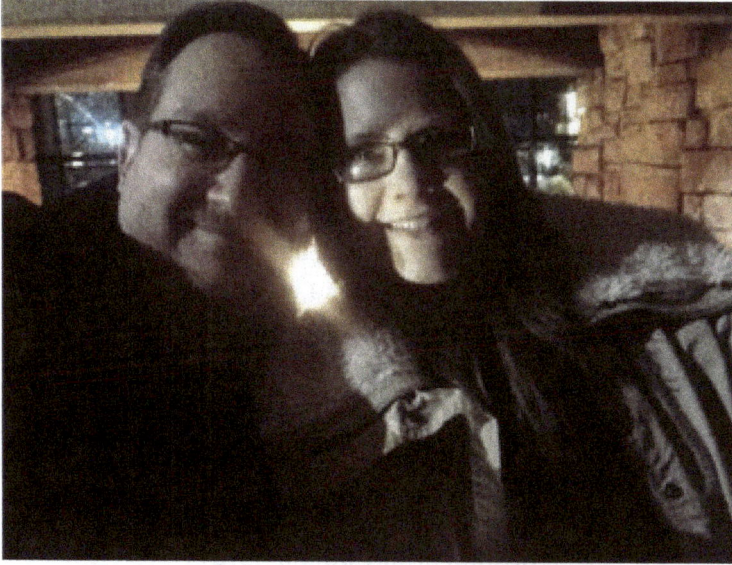

This picture was taken on the night Ethan and Liz
celebrated their last wedding anniversary together.

GRATITUDE

If there were no stars
To light the night sky;
No Father in heaven
To hear when we cry;

If darkness succeeded
In covering the sun;
Where could we go?
Oh, where could we run?

If there were no fragrance
In the heart of a rose;
No blush in the sunset
As day draws to its close;

If there were no memories
Of life's brightest days;
Where would we find comfort
Through grief's lonely haze?

If butterflies vanished
And birds sang no song;
And all of life's pathways
Were rocky and long;

If wintertime came
But refused to relent;
If spring no more budded
When winter was spent;

If no babies were born
And no eggs filled the nest;
Would the world turn in silence?
Content then to rest.

If rainbows didn't follow
The morning's soft rain;
And love freely given
Brought nothing but pain;

If one step wasn't followed
By another and more;
If courage had faltered
With none held in store;

How would we live
In a world such as this?
If all was denied us
Of sweetness and bliss;

Would we still find a way?
In loss and despair?
To brighten each day;
Or would we still care?

How thankful I am
For the stars that still shine;
For the birds singing sweetly
In a world still divine;

How grateful I am
For heavens above;
And darkness can't touch me;
I'm safe in God's love.   J.S. Schmidt 2-1-19

REMEMBER ME

The Lord Jesus the same night in which He was betrayed, took bread; And when He had given thanks, He brake it, and said, Take, eat: this is my body, which is broken for you: this do in remembrance of Me. After the same manner also He took the cup, and when He had supped, saying, this cup is the new testament in my blood: this do ye, as oft as ye drink it, in remembrance of Me. For as often as ye eat this bread, and drink this cup, ye do show the Lord's death till he come.

1 Corinthians 11

Today is Sunday morning, August 4, 2019. I attended church this morning; it happened to be Communion Sunday. As I walked down the aisle toward the place where the communion bread and the cup waited, I had a sudden revelation:

Three and a half years ago, in the crypt beneath the National Cathedral in Washington D.C., Jesus gave me a commission, a new purpose for my life and a way to heal my broken heart and spirit. When the officiant said these words: *"Whoever desires to come after Me, let him deny himself, and take up his cross and follow Me."*

Mark 8:34

I knew in that moment what I was being told to do with my life. I have thought about that moment many times since then, but never until today, did it dawn on me that Jesus had spoken to me, (through the words spoken by the officiant) in the midst of the ceremony He gave us to remember His great sacrifice for mankind. The greatest act of love ever recorded. I am so moved that Jesus chose that moment to show me the way forward, in my profound grief, was to love others, to help others, however I could and in doing so, be blessed with healing and a closer relationship with Him. I am reminded of these words of John Wesley:

Do all the good you can,
By all the means you can
In all the ways you can,
In all the places you can,
At all the times you can,
To all the people you can.

This is the commission Jesus gave to me on that day in the National Cathedral.

THE TOMB

The sun did rise;
That Easter morn;
Upon the city;
So forlorn.

Where Jesus suffered;
Bled and died.
Upon the cross;
Was crucified.

The tears of heaven;
At last were dried.
For Jesus rose;
And stood beside;
The tomb that could not hold Him.

Three women came;
That day at dawn;
With grief and sorrow;
They were drawn;

To that place of death;
Among the stone;
Where Jesus lay;
So cold and alone.

With heavy hearts;
They walked on still;
Among the rocks;
Along the hill;
To the tomb that could not hold Him.

And when they came;
To the place of rest.
They could not perform;
Their deathly quest.

The oils they brought;
Were useless now.
The Savior dead;
Had been reborn.

They found Him not;
Within the ground;
Nor in the rocks;
And hills around;
The tomb that could not hold Him.

Where can He be?
They asked in fear.
Then saw a gardener;
Standing near.

Who do you seek?
I beg of you?
A man called Jesus;
A man we knew.

Why do you seek;
The living here;
In this place;
Of death and tears?
In this tomb that could not hold Him.

He is not here;
He is not dead.
He walks the hills;
Alive instead.

Go spread the joy;
To all who cried;
To those who fear;
Who run and hide!

Tell His friends;
The things you know;
And He will come;
And prove it so;
For the tomb it could not hold Him.

And so it was;
As He had said:
"I'll be reborn;
After I'm dead;
To live again;
In heaven above."
A miracle;
Through God's great love.
And those of you;
Born in Me;
My Father's house;
Shall also see.

And though you lie;
Within the tomb;
And suffer death;
And earthly gloom;
The tomb it cannot hold you."
J.S. Schmidt- March 1989- Easter

I WILL ALWAYS LOVE YOU

I have previously written about my paternal grandmother and my bonus grandmother; this chapter touches on the life of my maternal grandmother, Marie Carlisle Tarpley. She was affectionately known in our family as Big Marie, even though she was a tiny woman. My mother, Marie, was her daughter and she was known as Little Marie. They were both less than 5ft. tall.

We saw Grandma Marie seldom as we grew up; she lived in Texas and every few years she would ride the bus from Dallas, to where we lived in Kansas to visit us. Her older sister, Anna, raised our mother from the age of about 3 yrs. old. Anna and Richie lived about a half a block away, on the same street and there were some bad feelings about all of that and suspicions, one of the other. Her visits often caused an uncomfortable undercurrent.

Grandma was very petite, rather pretty and stylish. I thought she looked like a slightly older version of my mother. Their sense of humor was the same and when they laughed, they sounded the same. She was a seamstress and always had pretty clothes; I always thought of her as sweet and kind. She married several times, and yet she spent the better part of her life living alone. She buried two husbands; the two she seemed to have been happy to be with. She decided happiness in marriage just wasn't meant for her.

As I write this, one of my husband's brothers lies critically ill in a hospital not far away. He is a young man; not as young as the son we lost, but young enough not to have lived a full life. It brings back many feelings I experienced following Ethan's passing; restlessness, uncertainty, sadness, and the queasy feeling that was with me for months. My grandmother comes to mind at this point, because she always prefaced any plan, she related to you by saying; *"If I live and do well, I'll..."* It's an old - fashioned saying people don't use anymore. People now just seem to assume they will go on living indefinitely. We are conditioned to believe there is a pill or procedure or miracle cure for anything that could possibly threaten our lives. Proverbs 27:1 says:" *Do not boast about tomorrow, for you do not know what a day will bring."* I say those words or a reasonably close paraphrase of them often, since Ethan's life was taken *"You never know what a day will bring."* Any day that you have all of your family with you, is a good day. Any day no one you love is sick or dying, is a good day. Never take for granted those you love; tell them what they mean to you, often. Never part from them in anger. Never forget to hug them or leave them with a kiss. When you are irritated with them;try to picture what your life would be like without them.

The last song we played at Ethan's celebration of life service was "Shower the People" by James Taylor. It was meant as a message of love from Ethan to all those people who were there to honor him and who he was. How grateful I am to know his last words to me were *"I love you"* and the last words I spoke to him, in this life were *"I love you."*

I recently visited the cemetery in the town my father grew up in; both of my parents are buried there, in fact, most of my Dad's large family is buried there. I stopped to visit my parent's gravesite, and then proceeded to drive down the narrow sandy lanes that led back to the entrance. My eye happened to catch some words written on the back of one of the grave stones and when I looked closer, I saw they were the words of Dolly Parton's song "I Will Always Love You". What an appropriate place to find them! Love never dies- In the end there is only Love.

RELEASE ME

As I near the end of this book, I realize there is one more thing I need to say. My grandchildren are all growing up and beginning to want to do things they may or may not be ready for, either physically, mentally, emotionally or spiritually. Their parents are sometimes emotionally conflicted about allowing them to go beyond what they perceive their limits to be. If you are the parent of grown children, this will all sound very familiar. We all want so desperately to make the right decisions regarding our children. It didn't take me very long to discover there were loads of things those parenting books didn't cover. On many occasions, you find yourself standing alone, without a clue as to what you should say or do. We want to give our children room to grow, but at a controlled and moderate rate. We want to give them space, but not more than is good for them. We want to let them try their wings, but we fear they might fall from the nest, rather than rise up on timid wings and fly. This is the awesome responsibility God entrusts to us when he gives us children; after all they are really His children, which He gives to us to love and nurture for a time, but ultimately, they return to Him. In essence, this is the price of the joy and love they bring to us as parents; we must one day let them go.

After Ethan's life was taken, I had the inevitable feelings of irrational guil,t that probably would plague any loving parent; I failed to protect my child and I lost him. My husband's feelings of guilt and failure were even more profound than my own. He sees himself as the protector of everyone he cares about. Our son was a nearly 40yr. old man; he wasn't a child living in our home. He wasn't even living in the same state. He had children of his own, that he felt the same sense of responsibility for, that we felt for him. In my case, those unreasonable emotions left me pretty quickly; I'm not sure my husband will ever truly leave them behind. Each of us deals with our grief in their own way and in their own time.

Ethan was an Assistant Professor of History, working to achieve tenure and full professorship. Teaching was the greatest love of his life; right after his love of family. He was always troubled in his heart, if he had to give a bad grade or caught someone cheating and had to report them. Ethan and I had at least two conversations about this and my concern was always that a student might become angry with him and return with a gun and hurt him. I know he fully understood that was a possibility, but he would always tell me how much he loved his job and it required him to be as fair to everyone involved as he could be, including those students who worked hard for a good grade and didn't resort to cheating. He would always say" *I just can't worry about things like that; I have a job to do."*

In the depths of grief, there is a moment, a very brief moment, when the pain of loss is so great, the thought crosses your mind, *"Perhaps, I should never have had this child."* It is only a millisecond before your heart rejects that thought and you realize the love and joy this child brought to your life, is worth any amount of pain you experience in losing him. When I ask myself if I would do it all over again, knowing what I know now; the answer is unequivocally, overwhelmingly, yes.

As a parent it is part of your responsibility to love your child enough to set them free. They must leave your side and go out into a dangerous and unwelcoming world and you must let them go with your blessing. I let Ethan go, believing (having faith), that he would be okay. Someone took his life, but I know, through the strength of my faith that he is more than okay; he just isn't physically here with us. God's protection doesn't mean our loved ones won't ever be gone from our earthly lives. It means their spirit can't be destroyed and they still live, beyond this world.

When I began to communicate with Ethan's spirit ,after his passing, I received this message:

"You gave me the freedom to grow up and leave your side, because your love for me outweighed your need to protect me, from everything that could hurt me. I know you were trying to trust that I would be okay; Well, I'm more than okay, I'm where I can never be hurt again. I know the physical separation is hard for you, but you know how close I really am.

Ethan

Butterfly
If you love something;
Set it free;
If it comes back to you;
It's yours;
If it doesn't;
It never was.
                    Richard Bach

A FINAL WORD

I thank you so much for reading "Roses and Thorns". I hope you have found inspiration, or at the least a word of encouragement. Writing is such a cathartic exercise for me and I believe God wants me to share these thoughts with others. I don't know what His purpose for that would be, but I don't question it. It may be that it's because it helps me and not someone else. If that be the case, thank you for indulging my need to express myself in this way. I also thank you from the bottom of my heart for reading the poetry. I know poetry isn't part of many lives these days, so I appreciate your indulgence there also. I've chosen to include a poem written by my oldest granddaughter, Taylor, in which she shared some of her thoughts about her Uncle Ethan and another written by Ethan's oldest son, Connor, as part of an English assignment in high school. I love both of them and their poetry; they come by it honestly!

J. S. Schmidt

WINGS

Carrying pollen from flower to flower,
They spread beauty and joy.
Each is an artist's masterpiece,
Made from all colors.
From the orange and black monarchs,
To the blue morphos,
Each is beautiful in its own unique way.
Chosen to carry the spirits of those loved,
They'll be seen when needed most.
With the wind, in the sky,
I know they've been sent to me by you.
When I'm running,
And about to give up,
You show up,
Flapping your wings and telling me to go on.
When I think it's all fallen apart,
You appear,
Reminding me of the good,
Wiping away my tear.
Whenever butterflies are near,
I always know you, Uncle Ethan, are near.

Taylor L. Schmidt

TEACHER

You showed me
Beauty has no bounds
Like a petal drifting in the wind
Moving but not making a sound
You showed me
To look closely
You never know what you may miss
You showed me
The love and compassion
A grandson needs
Ever since my first breath,
My first step,
And my first words
You have been my teacher

Connor D. Schmidt

WHEN

When all the world in silence lies
Beneath the dark and starless skies;
When humanity holds collective breath
And awaits with fear the final death;
When time and sound no more progress
And money and fame don't gain success;
When the skies shall split as we've been told
And love is all on earth we hold.

When Christ has come in raiment white
And darkness fails to quash the Light;
When all shall see Him face to face
And all the earth is a Holy place;
When He comes to restore the paradise lost
And wickedness shrinks from the sacred cost;
When earth is clean and bright and new
Each color restored to its heavenly hue;

Then shall we know the depth of love
The Savior brings from heaven above.
Then shall we see the depth of grace
The compassionate glow of Jesus' face.
Then shall we see the beauty bright
The heavenly host in glorious light.
Then shall we hear with ears unbound
The angel's song of praise profound.

Then, oh then, the sights we shall see
The unbridled joy there will then be;
When heaven comes down at last to earth
And all rejoice in the world's new birth.

                        J.S. Schmidt- Sept.9, 2018

CREDITS

SONG TITLES AND COMPOSERS/WRITERS

IN MY LIFE...Lennon/McCartney
WISH UPON A STAR...............................Harline /Washington
IN MY REPLY..Taylor
ANGEL BAND...............................Bradbury/Dadmun/Hascall
EARTH ANGEL.................................. Belvin/ Hodge/Williams
COUNT YOUR BLESSINGS.......................................Oatman Jr.
GIVE ONE HEART...Hall/Hall
LONESOME VALLEY... Guthrie
SUNRISE/SUNSET... Bock/Harnick
CITY OF NEW ORLEANS..Goodman
SUPPERTIME...Stanphill
WILL IT GO ROUND IN CIRCLES.......................Preston/Fisher
TWILIGHT TIME............................Dunn/Nevins/Nevins/Ram
ADAM AT THE WINDOW...McCarthy
CALLING MY CHILDREN HOME...........Yates/Waller/ Lawson
RAINY DAY PEOPLE..Lightfoot
CHURCH IN THE WILDWOOD...Pitts
BROTHER LOVES' TRAVELING SALVATION SHOW...Diamond
FLORA'S SECRET...Ryan/Bhraonain
I CAN SEE CLEARLY NOW...Nash
LEAVING ON A JET PLANE..Denver
SILVER WINGS..Haggard
ALL MY LOVIN'..Lennon/McCartney
ISLE OF ST. HELENA.. Traditional
WAITING FOR THE SUN TO SHINE...................Throckmorton
UNTIL THE TWELFTH OF NEVER...............................Webster
WHERE HE LEADS ME...Blandy
WALK THROUGH THIS WORLD WITH ME..Seamons/ Savage

GREAT IS THY FAITHFULNESS..................Chisolm/Runyun
THANK YOU LORD FOR YOUR BLESSINGS ON ME......Easter/
Easter
REMEMBER ME...Weil/Horner
RELEASE ME...Williams/Coffer
I WILL ALWAYS LOVE YOU....................................Parton

www.ingramcontent.com/pod-product-compliance
Lightning Source LLC
Chambersburg PA
CBHW051850090426

42811CB00034B/2278/J